Harley-Davidson

THE MAKING OF A CULT

Harley-Davidson

THE MAKING OF A CULT

Peter Henshaw

Photographed by Andrew Morland

LONGMEADOW
P R E S S

Cover design by Annabel Trodd
Interior design by Annabel Trodd
ISBN 0-681-45507-1
Printed in Italy
098765432

Harley-Davidson: The Making of a Cult is the
private view of the author and is not an official
Harley-Davidson publication.

JACKET
Front - Post-war Duo Glide, a typical 1950s
Harley
Rear - Black and chrome Duo Glide with all
the options

TITLE PAGES
Harley-Davidsons customized, personalized
and untouched

CONTENTS

INTRODUCTION

To begin with a cliché, Harley-Davidson is unique. The fact that you have bought this book means that you already know this. But it is far more interesting to speculate just why this all-American company, which started off as two men working in a shed, has not only survived, but prospered. Why is it, when so many other pioneer bikemakers have fallen by the wayside, this one is still treading a profitable independent path into the 1990s.

Plenty of Harley riders will wax lyrical about 'V-twin thunder', 'unique character', and all those little chromey bits. But there is more to it than that. There have been other bikes with both thunder and character to spare, yet they are no more. Take the Vincent, a classic V-twin from Stevenage in England. That had plenty of both, but in 1955 production ceased - there were just not enough people around rich enough to afford it. And therein lies one of the reasons for Harley's survival. It has always been a relatively affordable bike.

From the beginning, William Harley and the Davidsons (which makes them sound a bit like a '50s beat combo) aimed to make, not the fastest

bike, or the smoothest, or the most beautiful, but the most durable. One which would continue to give good service day after day on the rutted roads of early 20th century America. It was designed to appeal to the type of person who valued reliability above all; to be a regular workhorse rather than a rich man's weekend toy. It had to be cheap. By one of those fortunate coincidences, both Arthur Davidson and William Harley were talented engineers, and the eldest Davidson (another William) was a consummate cost controller. He was never a motorcyclist, but he was a real production man, of the breed that was to pioneer America's mass production industries in the late 19th/early 20th centuries. This tight control of production efficiency, and therefore of the product's cost, gave Harley-Davidson a headstart on less practical competitors. It allowed the company to survive the thin Depression years and beyond. Of course, the Japanese arrived to set new standards of technology and this is one of the reasons why Harley began to lose its traditional police contracts in the late '60s. But by then the cult had firmly established itself.

Nowadays, the notion of 'cult' is a somewhat misused concept. It has acquired negative connotations, associated more often than not with megalomaniacs posing as religious leaders. But a look inside the Oxford English Dictionary will reveal the true meaning of the word. 'System of religious worship; devotion or homage to person or thing (esp. derogatory of transient fad).' One could hardly describe the popularity of Harley-Davidson as a transient fad, though some would say that a religious devotion was not too far off the mark.

At the first Harley rally I ever attended, the handful of Japanese and British bikes was relegated to a little fenced-off compound. It was as if their presence might sully the pure Harley-Davidson-ness of the event. Inside, Harley hats, mugs, T- shirts, belts, buckles, key fobs, jackets, and probably underwear were much in evidence. Of course, every bike manufacturer has its followers - people have been wearing woolly hats with 'BSA' on them for years. But can you imagine a T-shirt with the slogan 'BSA's Best - F..... the Rest.' Or how about 'God Rides a Honda 125!' It doesn't have quite the same ring about it, does it? It is also said that the only reason God rested on the seventh day was because He had to spend all Sabbath maintaining His bike! There is an indefinable difference about Harley-Davidson and the cult it has inspired - but what is it?

To describe Harley as a piece of Americana is another cliché, but one in which there is an element of truth. We live in a world where symbols of American capitalism are recognizable just about everywhere - Coke, Macdonald's, Levi, brand names which have crept into everyday language.

This could be seen as cultural imperialism, a process whereby world cultures become ever more standardized to the American mould. If the process continues, every high street from China to Peru will end up selling Big Macs rather than the local delicacies, and a great part of the charm of foreign travel will be lost. Local customs and cuisine will be squeezed out, to the ultimate benefit of some 17th floor boardroom in Manhattan. Writing in the England of the 1990s, where fast food is becoming the norm and there is drive-in everything, this process appears already far advanced.

But does this have any relevance to Harley-Davidson? Well, yes it does. The company's recent world-wide success has really come on the back of other fashionable American exports. Harleys are selling fast in Europe and elsewhere not because they are faster or more comfortable than the opposition but because they are Harleys; they represent America. Now if this were not the case, and Harley-Davidsons were selling purely on engineering merit, the picture in Europe would be very different. The big, torquey V-twin would be seen as the perfect basis for a big, torquey cafe racer - White Power forks, grippy Avons and a lightweight frame by Ken Sprayson. But when European riders modify their Harleys (and most of them do) they do not try to Europeanize them. Instead, they add exactly what the American rider would - fancy paint, raked out forks, lots of chrome. In other words, they are emphasizing the American-ness of the product, and that is why they, and everyone else, buy, polish and worship the Harley-Davidson.

Harley has one big advantage in all this; no one else in America makes bikes. This was not always the case; the United

LEFT
Four Evo-mounted HOG members enjoy the sunshine at a rally near London, summer 1993

States once had a profusion of
pioneer motorcycle
manufacturers similar to those of
other Western nations. If Indian,
Excelsior and at least some of
the others were still in existence
today, Harley's place as the
ultimate American Freedom
Machine would be less clear cut.
But a combination of
mismanagement and Henry
Ford's T put the others out of
business. Indian managed to
hang on until the mid-'50s, but
since then, Harley has had the
America-on-two-wheels business
all to itself. Look at the way the
riders dress. You are extremely
unlikely to see anyone piloting a
Harley-Davidson in a blue nylon
rainsuit. Bandanas and black are
the order of the day. If any bike
required a uniform, this is the
one.

If part of Harley ownership
can be seen as a love of America
and things American, another
part can equally be considered a
symbol of rebellion. The need to
rebel manifests itself in everyone
from time to time and there is
something about the Harley
which satisfies that need. There
is something of the rebel, or at
least a desire to be different, in
every motorcyclist. This is more
often than not a bit of a personal
fantasy. While the black-garbed
biker, thundering through the
rain, may see himself as a
reincarnation of James Dean, a
bystander may wonder why on
earth he doesn't buy himself a
car and avoid getting wet. It is
true, though, that the emergence
of outlaw bike gangs after the
war, first in the United States,
then in Europe, centred on
Harley as the rebel's machine.
Films like *Easy Rider* and *The
Wild One* tended to reinforce

RIGHT
*All sorts of people, and all sorts of
Harleys, at a HOG Rally*

this image - Marlon Brando actually rode a Triumph for the cameras, but everyone seems to have forgotten this. It is tempting to dismiss Harley riders as weekend rebels, donning leathers and denims on Saturday to revert to collar and tie come Monday. This may be true of a few, but there are many other riders to whom Harley is a way of life.

* * *

For a company which has kept the same engine configuration for over 60 years, Harley-Davidson has produced quite a variety of models. The first bikes were singles, in the manner of every other utility machine of the time. In fact, the very first were not proper motorcycles at all, but motors fixed to a strengthened bicycle frame. As the frames broke, so they were redesigned heavier and stronger; consequently they needed bigger, more powerful engines to haul them along. And if you are already making a single, the simplest way to make a bigger version is to simply double it up as a V-twin. That way, you can even use the same head, barrel and piston assemblies. That is almost exactly how Harley made its first twin, the 35 cu inch single (around 570cc) became a 61-inch Vee. For some reason (anything to do with machine tools?) Harley-Davidson became very fond of certain engine displacements.

Take the 74, which started life in 1922 as an IOE engine, followed by the side-valve VL and OHV Panhead, all with the same capacity. As the 1940s gave way to the '50s and '60s, the OHV 74 was used on various bikes and their names affixed by 'Glide', with prefixes denoting major (for Harley) model changes. Thus Hydra Glide trumpeted the arrival of telescopic front forks, the Duo added rear suspension to that, the Electra electric start, and so on. In fact, the 74 became the mainstay of Harley's post-war range, lasting right up to the 1980s. After a short gap, it reappeared in Evolution Sportster form. Likewise, the biggest ever Harley production engine, the 80-incher, has remained the biggest in the line-up from side-valve to Evolution incarnations. If you believe that size is everything, it has since been overtaken by various Japanese pretenders, but Harley-Davidson has sensibly decided not to get caught up in a capacity race.

When the Evolution arrived in 1984, it was more like a revolution for many Harley-Davidson buffs. Even today, there are those who dismiss it as a Jap Harley. But from the outside, it was clear that this big step for the company was a very small one by everyone else's standards. The engine's bottom-end was basically that of the old Shovelhead, pure and simple. And even if the barrels and heads were all-new, they still used pushrods. But the new aluminium alloy top-end did represent a big advance. High oil consumption, whether through leaks or burning, was abolished. Power was up, emissions went down, and the engine could support a high(ish) compression ratio without overheating. Capacities, as ever, remained the same and, first appearing in the 80-inch top line Harleys, the new engine permeated downwards. Even the Sportster reverted to its original 883cc!

The Evo has of course attracted a whole new clientele into Harley ownership, but what the company has failed to do in the last decade is try to diversify downwards. Not that it did not try in the past. It is a measure of Harley-Davidson's V-twin-centred ethos that all of these baby bikes have been either heavily influenced by someone else's, or built by another firm altogether. The first attempt came early - a horizontally opposed twin appeared in 1919. Named the Sport Twin, and with more than a nod to the English Douglas, it was aimed at the gentleman rider who really did not fancy the tougher and rortier Vees. It only lasted three years. Then there were the inter-war singles, with side-valves or pushrods, 21 or 30.5 cu inches. The engine sizes again pointed to English influence, being the popular Old World 350 and 500cc. This time they were listed for five years before Harley-Davidson decided that small bikes were really not its thing.

The year 1947 marked the advent of the Hummer. This 125cc two-stroke was basically a German DKW design which came to Harley as part of the spoils of war. BSA took it over in exactly the same way to produce the Bantam. But like BSA, Harley-Davidson did very little to the engine apart from occasional capacity increases. It did quite well in the early '50s, but the later Japanese opposition made short work of it. Finally, came the Aermacchi bikes, Italian two- and four-strokes from 50 to 350cc. They were adopted as Harley-Davidsons following the company's takeover of Aermacchi when the Harley badge was fixed to their tanks. But in the end, Harley-Davidson have always returned to what they know best; pushrod V-twins.

RIGHT
Red, white and chrome

NEW BOYS MAKE GOOD

Not many people know that William Harley and Arthur Davidson, founders of the all-American motorcycle, although born in the United States, were of British descent. William's parents were originally from Manchester, England, and Arthur's from Aberdeen, in Scotland. Had the two families remained in Britain, and moved to, say, Coventry in the English Midlands, home of much of the United Kingdom's motorcycle industry, the Harley-Davidson might well have been a British bike.

But the Harleys and Davidsons did not stay at home. They chose to emigrate to a country which, at the turn of the century, still had enough energy and enthusiasm to deserve the epithet 'New World'. It was a young country with an expanding economy, dirt roads - and a crying need for transportation. So it was by a series of happy coincidences that the two families settled in Milwaukee, Wisconsin; that William and Arthur attended the same school and become firm friends; that they discovered a common interest in mechanics. By the first months of the 20th century, one innovation drew their attention above all others - the gasoline engine. No doubt young men all over the country were attempting their own version of the new motor. That Harley and Davidson succeeded where countless others were destined to fail could be attributed to basic characteristics which were to stand them in good stead in the turbulent years to come - practicality, commonsense and caution.

Arthur was the outgoing one. A patternmaker for the first bikes, he was to develop into a natural salesman and dealer recruiter. Bill Harley was more the technician, a draughtsman

who designed the early machines. They were soon joined by Walter Davidson the machinist. He built the bikes, but soon took on the administration and eventually became the first-ever President of Harley-Davidson Inc. The eldest Davidson, another William, came in later. An experienced toolmaker and foreman, he was the obvious choice for Works Manager in the rapidly expanding factory. These then, were the four founders, whose complementary skills were to get Harley-Davidson up and running, help it survive through difficult times, and mould its character for the future.

Bill and Arthur's first objective was not to make a motorbike at all, but rather to design a motor for their small fishing boat. They read around the subject, and things might have ended there, had not a German draughtsman named Emil Kroeger been able to supply them with technical drawings of the De Dion type engine. Harley and Davidson needed no second bidding, and their third prototype not only ran, but proved powerful enough to propel the boat. Fortunately for bikers everywhere, the two friends were also keen cyclists and a motorized bicycle was a natural progression.

That first prototype took three years to evolve into a practical road-going form, and at first differed little from countless similar contrivances. It was a standard heavy-duty bicycle frame with a tiny air-cooled cylinder bolted on. Harley-Davidson's first effort displaced just 10.2 cu inches, its flywheels were a puny 5 inches across, and the rider had to pedal up hills. There was an obvious answer, and the two responded with a bigger engine, more power and a purpose-designed frame. This marked Harley-Davidson's first

departure from the mass of motorized bicycle makers. They determined not to buy in engines and frames from outside, but to produce major components themselves. With 25 cu inches (just over 400cc) the new engine was bigger than its contemporaries, enough to give a top speed of 45mph.

Everything about this new machine was utterly conventional. The new frame was designed from the start specifically for a motorcycle, with a graceful loop as the lower tube to hold the engine. The wheelbase was lengthened and the whole thing built from heavy gauge tubing. Although the rest of it looked remarkably like a bicycle (right down to the unsprung front forks) it proved quite strong enough for those rutted roads. This was just as well - the first prototype's flimsy frame had a marked tendency to break, snap and distort. In this it was little different from many other motorized bicycles of the time. The difference was that the two partners determined to redesign the bike and get it right, rather than offload it straightaway on to a gullible public. So the new prototypes were test-ridden for miles, and when anything broke, it was strengthened. Thus the wheels acquired big rims, big hubs and big bearings and managed to stay in one piece. Drive was by a leather belt, which could be tightened or slackened to give a modicum of crude clutch slip, though the rider still had to pedal to get everything moving from rest.

So Harley and Davidson had a working machine, but it was still more part-time hobby than

RIGHT
Despite the technical advances, there was still only one colour scheme to be had around 1908; Harley-Davidson Gray

long-term business proposition. But by late 1903, several things happened that made the project far more serious. Walter Davidson had been working as a machinist in Kansas. Back home for the wedding of eldest brother William, he naturally tried out the bike. It must have made a big impression on him for he immediately threw over his old job and took one with the Chicago, Milwaukee and Saint Paul Railroad. That way, he would be able to live at home and work on the developing prototype in the evenings. The project was also outgrowing the family home and William C. Davidson, Scottish carpenter and father of the boys, decided to build a 10ft by 15ft wooden shed in the back garden. With 'Harley Davidson Motor Co' (it was to get the hyphen later) proudly painted on the door, it became the first factory. But, most significant of all, they received a first order for their 'Harley-Davidson'. They were in the motorcycle business.

* * *

For many budding young entrepreneurs, this would have been the cue to rush into production, but not the cautious team. Instead, in 1904, the Davidsons carefully built up just two more bikes (getting Aunt Jane to do the pinstriping) while Bill Harley went off to the University of Wisconsin. His engineering degree, financed by a part-time waiting job, was to prove invaluable when production began in earnest.

Things began to move faster now. The company decided not to advertize, but word was getting round that the quiet, solid Harley-Davidson, unlike many of its competitors, was reliable and stayed in one piece. The orders began to come in, and eight machines were built in 1905.

Walter abandoned his railroad job to work full-time in the wooden shed, with four part-time helpers. The shed was doubled in size, but within a year it had been outgrown again. A well-to-do Scots uncle, James McLay, lent them enough money to buy a plot of land on Chestnut Street (later Juneau Avenue), and Harley-Davidson had themselves a proper factory. In its first year, the new place produced 49 bikes.

All of these were virtual replicas of the original 1903 prototype, the 25cu inch engine

was no great innovation, but it was reliable, producing around 4bhp, a top speed of 45mph and (so it was claimed) up to 100mpg. Even if it drove through a crude, single speed leather belt, well, so did everything else at the time. The engine was a cross between overhead and side valve, with the inlet on top, the exhaust in a side pocket. Named inlet-over-exhaust (IOE), pocket valve or F-head, it became a Harley trademark. Something which did not last quite as long was the automatic inlet valve. Instead of a pushrod, the valve

relied on piston suction to draw it open, and compression (and a light spring) to close it. Even for 1906, it was hardly at the cutting edge of technology, and restricted the engine to around 300rpm. But like the rest of the bike, it worked, and went on working. This was the feature which really summed up the Harley ethos and which was to endure - Harley-Davidsons were solid and reliable.

LEFT
The first big twin gave around 11bhp, enough for 60mph out on the road

RIGHT
Final drive chain appeared in 1911 and three-speed transmission in 1915. For its time, the F was up-to-the-minute

BOTTOM RIGHT
Not the first Harley V-twin, but the first evolution of it; 1915 61ci F model

Production soared. It tripled in 1908 to 154 machines; increased to 450 the following year, then to over 1,000, then to over 3,000. By the start of the Great War, there were just two contenders for the title of biggest U.S. manufacturer - Indian and Harley-Davidson. It was an astonishing achievement, given that only 10 years had elapsed since those first, cautious beginnings. As factory space and workforce grew, Harley-Davidson came to need an experienced works manager. He arrived in the form of the eldest Davidson, William A. who joined the company in 1907.

The other three founder members had been anything but idle. Arthur began to pitch for public contract sales, to the mail carriers and police forces. He was starting to lay the foundations of a tradition which was to be associated with Harley-Davidson for many years. In 1908, Walter entered a single in the Federation of American Motorcyclists 180 mile Endurance Run. Typically, he had timed all his checkpoint arrivals with great care, and won easily. It was Harley-Davidson's first big break, and they

exploited the national publicity to the full. Meanwhile, Bill Harley had graduated, and returned to put theory into practice.

The single was still little changed from its original 1903 form, but a larger version was planned for 1909 when it was given a bigger 35 cu inch engine (now 5bhp and 50mph), leading link forks and a longer wheelbase. It still had that suction inlet valve and belt drive, but was at least moving with the times. The new 5-35, as it was known, did receive other updates in later life - pushrod inlet valve, chain drive, a clutch and two-speed gearbox all became available. But by this time it was overshadowed by a new Harley-Davidson, the V-twin.

*   *   *

For the first few years, there was little to differentiate American pioneer motorcycles from European ones, with their small De Dion type single cylinders. But travelled distances were greater in America, the roads were worse and motorcycles were fast taking on a utilitarian role. In other words they needed bigger

1903 single

SPECIFICATION	
Engine	Single cylinder, air-cooled, F-head type with automatic inlet valve and pushrod operated exhaust valve
Bore x Stroke	3 1/8 x 3 1/2in
Capacity	25ci
Piston	Solid skirt, 3 rings
Connecting rod	Automotive type with detachable big-end cap, big-end bush, small-end bush
Lubrication	Total loss, gravity fed via needle valve to crankcase
Starting	Bicycle pedals (hand crank optional)
Drive	Single speed belt drive from engine pulley to rear wheel. (Optional front pulley sizes of 4 1/2, 5 1/4 and 6in)
Clutch	None
Throttle	Right hand twistgrip
Brakes	Rear wheel only, by back pedalling
Wheelbase	51in
Tyres	Clincher, 2 1/4in cross-section
Weight	c 185lb
Suspension	None
Fuel capacity	1 1/2 gallons
Oil capacity	2 quarts
Fuel consumption	67-100mpg
Top speed	45mph
Finish	Black with gold striping, or grey with carmine striping
Price	$200

BELOW
Exposed valve gear needed frequent adjustment, though the total loss oiling was a trouble-free, if smoky, set-up

engines, and the easiest solution was a V-twin. A V could use a single's crankcase, suitably strengthened; it could use existing cylinder barrels; it would fit neatly into the bicycle-derived diamond frame. Best of all, the V-twin promised a virtual doubling of horsepower for only a small weight increase.

It is hard to believe now, but Harley-Davidson did not invent the V-twin. They were not even a pioneer: when Bill Harley started work on his version, he was merely following the trend of the times. Opinions differ as to when the new twin first saw the light of day, but it did not appear in the catalogue until 1909. As before, Harley's design broke little new ground. It used 5-35 cylinders (though with a smaller bore) with their F-head and automatic inlet valve. Incidentally, all the Harley F-heads had integral barrels and cylinder heads, which obviated gasket leaks but made for a complex casting. The smaller three-inch bore gave a capacity of 49.48 cu inches (811cc),

which drove through the same old leather belt.

It was not a success. Despite plenty of time to perfect the twin (it was apparently displayed in 1907), it was underdeveloped. The first 1909 model failed to have the expected power advantage, being still restricted by the automatic inlet valve. And what power there was was too much for the belt drive, which slipped badly. Under-development seemed to be becoming endemic in the Harley-Davidson company. New models were not appearing very often, and when they did, teething problems began to develop which should have been spotted earlier. This was in marked contrast to the founders' first efforts. In fact, it would seem that only two Harley-Davidson engines were properly developed before they went out on sale, the first single and the Evolution.

But in a year or so, the twin returned as the Model F, now with proper pushrod operation for the inlet valves and a

ABOVE
1923, and the big twin hasn't changed much, though this 61-incher had since been overshadowed by the new 74. Front- brake is a non-standard fitment

drive-belt tensioner. The capacity was still 49 cu inches, but was increased in 1912 to 61 cu inches. The first of Harley's familiar cylinder sizes had arrived. Otherwise, it was very similar to the abortive 1909 twin. Lubrication was still by gravity feed via a needle valve - apparently a drop every few seconds was about right. A supplementary hand pump came in later for those long, hot, hill climbs. The frame was based on that of the 5-35, but longer and heavier, while two options on the single (28-inch wheels and magneto ignition) were standard. In the electrical department, singles had the more modern-sounding battery, coil and points, but this was not as good as it sounded. There was no charging system at all, and it was necessary every so often to stop off at the drug store to buy new batteries. On paper, the F was not a great deal faster or more powerful than the single - Harley-Davidson claimed around 7bhp and 65mph - but the twin's real advantage was in lots of torque and more relaxed progress.

So, of course, it had what was necessary to haul a sidecar, which made motorcycling far more attractive to the family man as well as to mail carriers. From 1914, it was possible to order a Harley-Davidson sidecar to go with your smart new twin for just $85. In passenger format, it was quite a handsome piece of equipment, with its tapered nose, leather quilted seat and spray painted finish. Just as significant were the commercial sidecars. In 1915, they were authorized for Rural Free Delivery (Arthur's sales efforts had paid off) which opened up a huge market. Harley-Davidson also developed van bodies on sidecar chassis, which could carry up to 600 lbs. Harley-Davidson was certainly well aware of the commercial market. As well as the conventional sidecars, there was the Fore car. First appearing in 1913, this three-wheeler had a front axle and large box where the motorcycle's front wheel would have been. It was superseded by the famous Servi-Car, which was the same idea back to front - conventional front end, with the rear wheel replaced by a box on wheels. It was hardly surprising that over 16,000 sidecars were sold in 1919 - in other words, seven for every ten bikes. This was the golden age of the 'chair', of whatever make. But its heyday was briefer in the United States than elsewhere.

A man called Henry Ford was responsible. In 1909, you could buy four Harley singles for the price of his Model T. By the end of World War I, the T cost less than a good V-twin with sidecar, which effectively killed off the motorcycle as family transportation. It did not kill the motorcycle of course, but it did change its nature. Increasingly, and especially in the case of big Vees, motorcycles were bought not because they were cheap, but because they were exciting. Enthusiasts were beginning to filter into the growing market, and like everyone else, Harley-Davidson was forced to take notice.

But if the motorcycle market was changing, so was its technology. Some would argue that technical change was very rapid up to the early '20s, when it reached something of a plateau. Judging by the speed with which Harley-Davidson was beginning to improve its bikes, this was certainly true of the period from 1911 to 1916. With its pushrod inlet valves, 1911 saw the re-introduced twin and the following year, all Harleys got a new frame which had moved further away from the diamond-type bicycle look-alike. More significant, perhaps, was the arrival of chain drive. The leather belt, the cause of so much hassle for early riders, was on its way out at last.

1915 Model 11J

SPECIFICATION

Engine	Air-cooled IOE 45-degree V-twin, one-piece cylinders and heads
Bore x stroke	3 5/16 x 3 1/2in
Capacity	60.33ci (988cc)
Valves	Pushrod operated
Connecting rods	Knife and fork type, roller big-end bearing, small-end bush
Lubrication	Total loss, automatic engine-driven pump supplemented by hand pump
Carburettor	Schebler
Ignition	Bosch magneto
Starting	Step start, or bicycle pedals
Drive	Primary chain, final chain
Clutch	Dry, multiplate
Throttle	Right-hand twistgrip
Frame	Double bar loop, all joints brazed
Brakes	Rear only, internally expanding drum, operated by right pedal
Wheelbase	59 1/2in
Tyres	22 x 3in (G & J, Morgan & Wright, Goodyear or Goodrich)
Weight	325lb
Suspension	Front - leading link forks with 16 1/2in main spring, 4 1/2in recoil spring; Rear - none
Fuel capacity	1 7/8 gallons
Oil capacity	5 pints
Fuel consumption	c 50mpg
Top speed	c 60mph

Harley-Davidson even provided *in situ* lubrication for the new transmission - a breather in the timing case forced oil mist out of a tube onto the chain. Then there was the new clutch of Bill Harley's own design. Finally, although there was no rear suspension, the rider was made slightly more comfortable with the introduction of the Ful-Floteing saddle, which incorporated a 14-inch spring inside the seat tube.

There was something of a lull in 1913, though the twins now had roller bearing big-ends, while refinements like chain drive and mechanical inlet valves reached the singles. The year war broke out though, the step (what we would call a kick) starter appeared, which spelt the beginning of the end for those

bicycle pedals. And there was even a choice of gear ratios - the new two-speed rear hub transmission was a simple unit based on three sets of bevel gears, controlled by a lever on the left side of the tank. The singles got the roller bearing big-ends, and the twins' exhaust valve springs were enclosed - the exposed inlet valve gear still needed adjustment every 800 miles though. Several important new features appeared in 1915, most obvious of which was a three-speed transmission, located conventionally behind the engine rather than in the rear hub. A complete Remy electrical system, with magneto, battery, generator and lights, was offered as an alternative to gas lights. With gas, the twin was known as the F model; in electric form, it was the J, which in certain forms was to become one of Harley's longest lived and best loved models. There were numerous improvements to the V-twin, mainly to increase power - larger inlet ports, manifold and

carburettor, larger big-end bearings and an automatic engine-driven oil pump. The idea of the pump was to prevent the under- or over-oiling which came with the gravity-fed/hand pump system. In fact, over-oiling was the more common problem - anxious owners would overdo it on the hand pump, which led to overheating. Consistent, predictable lubrication helps power, and Harley-Davidson felt able to guarantee 11bhp from every V-twin, and even claimed to have seen 16.7 from one example. These were the last major changes to the F-head engine. Much had changed since the first 25 cu inch single of 1903, but that was just as well - the F-head was to remain the mainstay of the Harley-Davidson range for yet another 15 years.

Harley-Davidson did well out of World War I. That is not to say that they profiteered, but the founders did take a longer term view than Indian. When War Department contracts began to flow in 1916, it was Indian which offered most of its production to the Government at a low price. Harley-Davidson, on the other hand, took the precaution of retaining half for the domestic civilian market. The result? Lots of disgruntled Indian dealers with no bikes to sell. Arthur lost no time in recruiting these malcontents, which greatly strengthened Harley-Davidson's position in the home market. Sharp business practice, perhaps, but in the long-term good for the company which was able to challenge Indian for market leadership. It also, no doubt, helped to foster the intense rivalry between the two leading motorcycle manufacturers. As for the bikes, there was very little difference between civilian and military type Harley-Davidsons, many of which found their way back to civvy street after the war. Despite the fact that they supplied less than half the

number of bikes that Indian did, Harley managed to claim attribution for the story (used to great effect in later years) that Corporal Roy Holtz, the first American soldier to enter Germany, did so on a Harley-Davidson sidecar outfit!

Milwaukee (as the company was also often known) exited the war in confident mood. The J series twins were well-established and popular, the dealer network was stronger than ever, and the company was a now serious challenge to Indian. So in an uncharacteristic fit of optimism, the founders borrowed over $3 million from the bank, which they spent on doubling capacity and the latest machine tools. Completed in April 1920, the vast new factory addition was large enough for 2,400 employees and the

production of 35,000 bikes a year. It was a bad move. The following year the economy, now without the artificial prop of war production, collapsed. So did motorcycle sales, and Harley sold little more than 10,000 bikes in 1921 - the lowest figure for a decade.

But all this was still in the future, and the new confidence was still abounding so that in 1919, Harley astonished everyone with a piece of lateral thinking. Their new middleweight twin had unit construction, an enclosed chain - and it was not a Vee. The inappropriately-named Sport Twin was an attempt to open up the gentleman motorcyclist market for people who wanted cheap, fuss-free transport, but nothing too utilitarian. The Sport, or WJ, was

ABOVE
Twin headlights (here on a 1929 J) only lasted a year, which was a pity

Sport Twin

SPECIFICATION

Engine	Horizontally opposed twin, side valve
Bore x stroke	2 3/4 x 3in
Capacity	35.6ci (584cc)
Compression ratio	c 3.75:1
Power	6bhp
Carburettor	Schebler
Lubrication	Automatic oil pump
Gearbox	Three-speed sliding gear, unit construction
Clutch	Wet, multiplate
Drive	Primary - helical gears Final - fully enclosed chain
Frame	Keystone type
Wheelbase	57in
Wheels	20in
Tyres	20 x 3in
Suspension	Front - trailing link with compression spring Rear - none
Fuel capacity	2 3/4 gallons
Oil capacity	2 pints
Finish	Brewster Green, striped in gold
Weight	250lb
Seat height	29 1/2in
Top speed	c 50mph
Fuel consumption	c 70mpg

Harley-Davidson's idea of what these people wanted.

Bearing more than a passing resemblance to a Douglas, it was a horizontally opposed twin of 36 cu inches, with the cylinders arranged fore and aft. Side valves, a very strange inlet valve angle and extraordinarily long inlet tract ensured that performance was far from stunning. With a claimed 6bhp on tap, it seldom reached the advertized 50mph, little more than the old 35 cu inch singles. It would be hard to imagine a machine more further removed from the rorty V-twins - gear primary drive, wet clutch, keystone frame. In the latter, the engine/gearbox was a stress-bearing member, bolted to the frame at each end. And the forks, rather than Bill Harley's time-honoured leading links, were trailing links.

There was actually little wrong with the Sport in itself. It was lightweight (just 265 lb), quiet and economical, though even the most placid of commuters might have wished for a little more speed. In Europe, where they appreciate these things more, the bike did quite well and earned some useful export revenue for Harley-Davidson. But in the United States it failed for two reasons. By this time, the V-twin was established as *the* enthusiast's machine; nothing else would do. In any case, Indian had fought back with the Sport Scout, a middleweight V-twin with more power and appeal than the WJ. Even more damning than that, a Model T cost only $15 more than the Sport in 1920. It is hardly surprising that it was dropped from the range after four years.

Just before Harley-Davidson dropped the Sport, they brought out something far more conventional - the Seventy-Four. Basically a 61-inch J twin with

larger bore and stroke, it was really a response to the Henderson Four and Indian Chief. For only $25 on the price of the 61-inchers, buyers could have one of the largest bikes on the market. Dubbed the Superpowered Twin by its makers, the 74-inch/1200cc J marked the debut of another of Harley-Davidson's famous

capacities. Apart from a few internal changes, the Seventy-Four just had a larger carburettor to distinguish it from its little brother. With the long stroke, the new bike majored on torque rather than power. The extra speed was to be much appreciated by illicit booze runners, who in those Prohibition days needed something capacious and accelerative on their nighttime journeys.

By 1928, the J series twins were starting to look decidedly old hat. Newer side valve Indians were just as fast, yet cheaper, but Harley's response was not too far away. It came with the Two Cam. Nothing as radical as twin camshafts, but four lobes (rather than two) to operate the four valves. The system had actually been seen

on competition Harleys since the end of the war, but never on road bikes. Its advantage over the traditional Harley use of the same cam for both inlet and exhaust was obvious. There was far more freedom in valve timing, and tappets could act directly off the cam, rather than via rev-limiting rockers.

It certainly transformed the J twins - the 74-inch JDH could top 85mph in standard trim, and some said it could breach 100mph with 'tender loving care'. Magnesium alloy pistons and higher compression came as part of the package. So it was little wonder that Harley-Davidson introduced front wheel brakes in 1928. The 61- and 74-inch two cammers cost a hefty $50 more than the single cams, which continued. But they were fast and powerful, just the thing to help Harley-Davidson combat the big Indian and straight four Henderson. Indeed, some riders thought it was the best thing they ever did.

ABOVE
Tank-mounted speedo is a sign of things to come. Note three-speed handchange

FALL...AND RISE

No one escaped the effects of the Wall Street Crash. At first, an optimistic public thought swift action by Herbert Hoover had saved the situation. But by the beginning of the 1930s, the worldwide scale of the economic slump became obvious. Statistics can never tell the true story; what it is like to be unemployed with a large family to feed, but there are a few pointers. In the United States, over 5,000 banks failed, one third of the railroads were bankrupt and 30 per cent of the workforce had no job.

In a world where motorcycling had increasingly become a leisure activity for the well-off young men of the '20s, and where a second-hand Model T could be picked up for $20, bike sales slumped. For most, motorcycling was not one of life's priorities; so it suffered. At the lowest point, less than 100,000 bikes were registered in the United States.

Take Harley-Davidson. Production had peaked at over 28,000 in 1920, though this had fallen to just over 17,000 V-twins by the end of the decade. In 1930 the fall was small, but in 1931 only 10,500 bikes were built, and in 1932, less than 7,000. The low spot came in 1933, when only 3,703 Harley-Davidsons were sold in America. With the whole world at a low ebb, there were few export sales to add to that, and 1933 saw its lowest production since 1910. It is therefore hardly surprising that talk of closure came up at Board meetings.

But Harley did not close and even emerged as a market leader by the end of the '30s. The long battle with Indian had finally been resolved. That is not to say that it was all plain sailing. There was no lack of new models, but Harley-Davidson was rarely right the first time round.

It seemed that whenever Harley-Davidson attempted to diversify, innovation was not its first priority. The Sport Twin looked very similar to the Douglas, while the inter-war singles also owed much to equivalent British motorcycles. Later still, of course, Harley was to take the ultimate step and put its badge on someone else's bike. But more of that later. The new singles announced in 1925 do not seem to have been part of a long-term plan to re-enter the market for little bikes. According to Harry Sucher, the 21-inch 'Peashooter' was more a response to arch-rival Indian. Indian itself, on hearing that Cleveland, the only successful U.S. lightweight of the time, was to drop its little bike, came up with a 21-inch side-valve in 1925. It is an indication of the intense rivalry between the two makers that Harley-Davidson had an equivalent out within a year. Examples of the new Indian Prince as well as a 350cc BSA and a New Imperial, were wheeled into Milwaukee's engineering department, and work began.

The result was actually two bikes; 21 cu inch singles with either side or overhead valves, making it hard to see why Sucher described them as scaled down J models. The frame was naturally all-new, though it did bear a resemblance to that of the big twins, right down to the patented spring seat post. Throughout the 21-inchers, the emphasis was on simplicity - three-speed hand change gearbox, dry clutch. Meanwhile, Harley claimed that decarbonizing the head took only 20 minutes from start to finish. This of course was a novelty for Harley-Davidson riders - the heads were not removable on any of the old IOE bikes. Reinforcing the English influence, those cylinder heads

were designed by Harry Ricardo. Famous for his work in this field, Ricardo's association with Harley had begun several years earlier on an eight-valve racer. The company was completely open about this, and paid royalties to the English designer. In truth, this was probably a good marketing move. Ricardo's standing was high in European motorcycling circles, and for a bike designed with exports in mind, his name added credibility to an American machine.

Not that the side-valves were fast. With just 8bhp at their disposal, the top speed was around 50mph, but trying to keep up 45mph plus invariably led to piston seizure. Apart from that, it proved to be pretty reliable, and many ended up carrying Western Union messenger boys. Two models were available - the magneto-equipped 'A', with its outmoded acetylene lights, and the all-electric 'B', which boasted a battery and generator system. The A was priced to sell at $210, though you only had to fork out another $25 for proper electrics.

The OHV bikes made far more impact, boasting 50 per cent more power (though strangely, this was quoted at the same 4,000rpm as the side-valves) which translated into 65mph capability and a cruising speed of 60mph. It was just a pity that the valve gear was exposed, needing frequent manual lubrication or adjustment; preferably both. Naturally, the zippier AA and BA cost more than the side-valvers; $250 with acetylene, or $275 with electric lights. They did well in competition too, both overseas and at home. The American

Motorcycle Association (Harley-dominated, it has to be said) instituted a 21 cu inch class, and Harley-Davidson's Peashooter swept the board. This was partly due to lack of competition - Indian made very few 21 cu inch Princes. So successful was the bike that Harley-Davidson produced a lightweight competition version - telescopic forks, shorter wheelbase and an all-up of just 215lb. More significant, the Peashooter's potential brought the near-genius of Joe Petrali into the Harley fold. A tremendously gifted rider in all forms of competition, Joe was also an excellent development engineer. His work was instrumental in bringing further competition success to Harley-Davidson.

If the 21-inchers owed a lot to European influence, the 1928 C model was closer to Harley's own idea of how a single should be. It was basically half a 61-inch V-twin, with long stroke, side-valves and very limited performance. The result should have been slow but reliable. Unfortunately, as well as sharing the 21-inch side-valve tendency to overheat and seize, it used the smaller bike's clutch and gearbox too. The C did not produce a lot of power, but it was still too much for the transmission. Opinions differ on the frame. Some say it started out with the 21-inch frame, later using the heavier 45 cu inch; others say it used the 45 cu inch right from the start. Harley's 500 lasted until 1936, but like its little brother, it was always overshadowed by the Vees.

If the 21-inch singles were a direct response to an Indian initiative, this was no more then standard Harley-Davidson policy at the time. The Wigwam was Harley's only true rival, and the management sometimes seemed obsessed with wresting market

A and B single models

SPECIFICATION

Engine	Single cylinder, air-cooled, side-valve (A, B) or overhead valve (AA, BA)
Bore x stroke	2 7/8 x 3 1/4in
Capacity	21.1ci (346cc)
Carburettor	Schebler Deluxe
Lubrication	Mechanical pump, supplemented by hand pump
Power	A/B - 8bhp @ 4,000rpm AA/BA - 12bhp @ 4,000rpm
Gearbox	Three-speed, sliding gear, hand change
Clutch	Dry, multiplate
Drive	Primary - chain Final - chain (5 5/8 x 1 1/4in)
Ignition	A/AA - Bosch magneto B/BA - Harley-Davidson battery and coil
Electrical eqpt	Harley-Davidson generator, coil, timer-distributor, battery, horn, twin bulb headlight, tail-light, ignition/light switch panel, battery/generator circuit controlled by relay cut-out
Brakes	Front - None Rear - External contracting drum (5 3/4in dia)
Frame	Tubular steel cradle type
Wheelbase	55in
Wheels	Clincher
Tyres	3.30 x 20in
Suspension	Front - Leading link Rear - None
Fuel capacity	3 gallons
Oil capacity	3 quarts
Weight	A - 251lb AA - 245lb B - 269lb BA - 263lb
Seat height	28 1/2in
Fuel consumption	c 50mpg overall
Top speed	A/B - c 50mph AA/BA - c 65mph
Finish	Harley-Davidson olive green with maroon and gold striping
Price	A - $210 B - $235 AA - $250 BA - $275

leadership from it. Matters became extremely tense in the early '30s. Just as Indian were

about to collapse, and leave Harley-Davidson with a virtual monopoly, it was saved by the

C model single

industrialist E. Paul du Pont. Dealers were often forbidden from servicing the rival - some even refused to serve 'enemy' customers. For a time Harley even chased prestigious police sales by offering its bikes at knock-down prices and destroying any Indians which might be traded in. It was not a happy time as excessive competition never benefits anyone. Strangest of all, while this was going on, the top brass of each firm would meet secretly to decide on the pricing of equivalent machines. This price fixing was of very little benefit to the customer, but it suited Harley-Davidson and Indian just fine.

All this was still in the future when Harley's 45 cu inch twin appeared in 1928. It was of course in response to the Indian Scout, a lively 45-incher which had been introduced earlier in the year and was selling well. That the 45 (and the new VL

SPECIFICATION

Engine	Single cylinder, air-cooled side-valve
Bore x stroke	3 $^{3}/_{32}$ x 4in
Capacity	30.5ci
Power	10.5bhp @ 3,600rpm
Carburettor	Schebler Deluxe, $^{7}/_{8}$in
Lubrication	Throttle controlled mechanical pump
Ignition	Harley-Davidson battery and generator
Electrical eqpt	Harley-Davidson generator, coil, battery, horn, two bullet headlights, single tail light, ignition/light switch panel with ammeter, battery/generator circuit controlled by relay cut-out
Gearbox	Three-speed sliding gear
Clutch	Dry, multiplate
Drive	Primary - chain ($^{3}/_{8}$ x $^{3}/_{4}$in) Final - chain ($^{5}/_{8}$ x $^{3}/_{8}$in)
Tyres	3.85 x 25in (1929 size)
Frame	Tubular steel cradle type
Wheelbase	56 1/2in
Fuel consumption	c 45mpg
Top speed	c 60mph
Finish	Harley-Davidson olive green with maroon and gold striping

27

twins) was a side-valve when OHV was the coming thing seems puzzling, especially as the 21 cu inch singles had demonstrated that Harley-Davidson knew how to make pushrod engines. The answer lay in Indian. Its 45 cu inch Scout and 61/74 Chiefs were all side-valves, and where the Wigwam went, Harley seems to have followed.

The 45's early career was not an auspicious one. Despite its tag 'Baby Harley', it was no lightweight at over 400lb, and the side-valve engine was in a very low state of tune. The result was hardly electrifying - one dealer ran-in his new demonstrator only to find it could not be coaxed beyond 56mph. And there were the 45 sidecar outfits supplied to the Yellowstone and Zion Park rangers. Performance was so feeble the chairs had to be taken off. The 45's limp output was partly by design - small carburettor, restrictive manifold and low compression - but rationalization played a part too. The 45 actually used the same clutch and gearbox as the little singles, so there was probably reason behind its modest power. For the record, the D put out 15bhp,and the higher compression DL about 18.5. An Indian Scout, with its shorter stroke, revvier nature and stronger gear primary drive, was altogether more attractive.

Matters improved in 1931, when the 45 gained its own more substantial frame and forks, but still it was by no means the fastest thing on the

RIGHT
Harley's longest-lived model (1932-1974) the Servi-Car was a uniquely American institution. This 1965 version is ex-North Carolina police

INSET
Low compression 45-in side-valve was lifted from the two-wheelers

D model V-twin

ABOVE AND RIGHT
Low mileage on this rare ex-police
example, seen at the Shaftesbury V-twin
rally in Dorset, England

SPECIFICATION

Engine	Air-cooled side-valve 45-degree V-twin
Bore x stroke	2 ³/₄ x 3 ¹³/₁₆in
Capacity	45.3ci (747cc)
Compression ratio	D - 4.3:1
	DL - 5:1
	DLD - 6:1
Power	D - 15bhp @ 3,900rpm
	DL - 18.5bhp @ 4,000rpm
	DLD - 20bhp @ 4,000rpm
Carburettor	Schebler Deluxe
	D - ³/₄in dia
	DL & DLD - ⁷/₈in dia
Lubrication	Total loss. Throttle controlled mechanical pump
Ignition	Harley-Davidson battery and coil
Electrical eqpt	Harley-Davidson generator, coil, 22amp/hr battery, horn, two bullet headlights, single tail-light, ignition/light switch panel with ammeter, generator/battery controlled by relay cut-out
Gearbox	Three-speed sliding gear
Drive	Primary - chain (³/₈ x ³/₄in)
	Final - chain (⁵/₈ x ³/₈in)
Clutch	Dry, multiplate
Suspension	Front - Leading link forks
	Rear - None
Wheelbase	57 ¹/₂in
Wheels	4.00 x 18in, quickly detachable, interchangeable
Tyres	3.85 x 18in
Weight	390lb
Seat height	26 ¹/₂in
Fuel capacity	3 ³/₄ gallons
Oil capacity	7 ¹/₂ pints
Fuel consumption	c 60-75mpg
Top speed (claimed)	D - 60-65mph
	DL - 65-70mph
	DLD - 70-75mph
Finish	Harley-Davidson olive green with maroon and gold striping
Price (1930)	$295

road. On the other hand, it was reliable. This was why it formed the basis of the WLA, the wartime Harley, and actually lived on to 1974 powering the Servi-Car.

The three-wheeled Servi-Car, with its motorcycle front end and two wheel rear axle, is remembered as a Harley invention. But as ever, Indian was there first. Well, that is not strictly true, as Harley-

Davidson's man in Japan, Alfred Rich Child, had been importing Harleys to the Far East, and converting them to the Servi-Car format since the mid-'20s. In the United States though, Indian's Dispatch-Tow did precede Harley-Davidson - it was aimed at the car repair business. The mechanic would ride out to the customer's house, hitch his Dispatch to the rear bumper, and drive car and bike back to the workshop. It was a good idea, and Harley-Davidson's first attempt to emulate this was the Cycle-Tow, which simply consisted of two fold-out wheels on either side of the standard bike's rear wheel. Introduced in 1930, not many Cycle-Tows were sold and it was soon withdrawn.

But a couple of years later, the Servi-Car proper appeared. More adaptable than its predecessor, its rear box could handle light deliveries; parking patrols liked its ease of use; the police liked its manoeuvrability; and of course, mechanics used it to collect and deliver customers' cars. It did, of course, use the 45-inch engine in lowest of the low tunes - but that was just what was needed when towing a heavy Chevvy back to the workshop.

The careful reader will have noticed something common to all of the last few specification tables - Harley-Davidson olive green. This drab shade had first appeared during the Great War, and had stayed ever since. Although from the late '20s comparatively exotic alternatives such as azure blue and cream had been optional, unless you specified to the contrary, your new Harley would arrive in olive green drab with the name on the tank picked out in sensible block capitals. Changing fashions, and the necessity for economic survival, brought a welcome change in 1933. Silver and turquoise for the singles, a wide choice on the twins, and they all got a beautiful art deco bird

V model

SPECIFICATION

Engine	Air-cooled, side-valve 45-degree V-twin
Bore x stroke	V/VL - 3 $^7/_{16}$ x 4in
	VLH - 3 $^7/_{16}$ x 4 1/4in
Capacity	V/VL - 73.7ci (1207cc)
	VLH - 80ci (1340cc)
Carburettor	Linkert
Lubrication	Total loss. Throttle controlled mechanical pump. (From 1937, recirculating dry sump)
Compression ratio	V - 4:1
	VL - 4.5:1
Power	V - 27bhp @ 4,000rpm
	VL - 30bhp @ 4,000rpm
Ignition	Harley-Davidson battery and coil
Gearbox	Three-speed sliding gear. Reverse or four- speed optional
Drive	Primary - chain
	Final - chain
Clutch	Dry, metal multiplates
Frame	Tubular steel cradle type
Wheelbase	60in
Wheels	Quickly detachable, interchangeable
	Front - 4.00 x 19in
	Rear - 4.40 x 19in
Tyres	4.00 x 18in (4.00 x 19in optional)
Suspension	Front - Leading link forks
	Rear - None
Weight	529lb
Seat height	28in
Fuel capacity	c 4 gallons
Oil capacity	8 $^3/_4$ pints
Fuel consumption	35-50mpg
Top speed	V - 80mph (est)
	VL - 85mph (est)
	VLH - c 100mph

motif. No wonder the mid-'30s Harley-Davidsons are considered the best-looking of all.

The early '30s was really Harley's side-valve period. It was probably that Indian influence again, whose side-valvers were out-performing Harley-Davidsons on road and track. The V series was really the culmination of all this - an all-new OHV twin was on its way, but was not yet ready,

while Harley needed something fast to top out the range.

Launched in 1930, the V was a direct replacement for the long-running IOE twins. It featured a new, more substantial frame and boasted 30 per cent more power than the old model. But soon after the first bikes were shipped out to dealers, it became clear that something was wrong. The supposed power advantage was not anything like 30 per cent, and the new bike weighed about

100lb more than the J. But what most people seem to have taken exception to was the small, light flywheels. These gave good acceleration up to around 50mph, but performance then fell off badly. Hill climbing and load lugging disappointed as well.

So loud were the protestations from dealer and customer alike that Harley-Davidson launched into a crash programme of major modifications. The result was larger flywheels, which needed larger crankcases, and in turn, a deeper frame loop. It all cost a lot of money, but in typical Harley fashion, the company merely sent the modified parts out to the dealers and told them to get on with the job at their

own expense. Anyone who protested faced the loss of their franchise. In all, over 1,300 machines had to be completely dismantled and rebuilt.

This debacle led many to conclude that the V was never the performance equal of the good old J series, particularly the last two-cammers. But, as ever, rose-tinted spectacles distorted the view. It is true that the V produced little more power than the IOE bikes, but it did have more torque in the upper rev range. Just as important, and unlike the two-cammers, the V could be cruised long and fast without falling apart. So it turned out right in the end. But the V (and those early 45 problems) did raise questions about Harley's testing of prototypes; in other words, did they do any?

No matter, Like the 45, the 74 cu inch (VL was the high compression version) evolved into a reliable bike, which succeeded in filling the performance gap until the new overhead valver arrived. There were those who wanted still more torque though, and the answer came in late 1935 with an 80 cu inch version, the VLH. Another of Harley's famous engine sizes had arrived. It was just the thing if you wanted to haul a sidecar. And anyway, Indian were making one.

BELOW
Olive green finish for this 1932 twin, though in theory, maroon, gray, cream, another green and two shades of blue could be ordered

BACK IN FRONT

Every motorcycle manufacturer has one model which represents a major breakthrough in its history. It might be faster than what went before, more reliable or better looking; above all, it might be different in concept, entirely new. There are various contenders for best European example, though Triumph's 1937 Twin Speed is the strongest. But in America there can only be one - the Harley-Davidson Knucklehead.

Not only was the 61E (to use its official title) twice as powerful as the old 61 and a stunning looker, its real significance for Harley-Davidson was that it formed the basis of every OHV Harley engine since. That is not to say that it has much in common with an Evolution, but since 1936, all V-twins have been modifications, rather than all-new.

By the mid-1930s, the Harley-Davidson was in danger of becoming an old man's motorcycle. With the reliability problems of those early 45 and 74 side-valvers finally solved, the range was settling into the tourists' choice. Harley-Davidsons were reliable and comfortable as well as long-lived; but they were also slow and heavy plodders. The Indians, by contrast, although not as well made, were fast - a Sport Scout could make mincemeat of Harley's 45. So it was all due credit to the four founders (all now nearing retirement age) that they bit the bullet and gave the go-ahead for an all-new overhead valve bike.

There had been OHV Harleys before, of course, both on road and track, but never before on a road-going V-twin. Work began in 1931, and the Board gave its approval in August of that year. This was commendable, not just for the technical innovations (by Harley-Davidson standards) that

it would involve, but for the timing of the decision taken in the midst of a slump with motorcycle sales at rock bottom. For 1932, planned production was cut to 9,000 bikes, less then half that for 1930. In the event, they made only 6,800. There were redundancies and pay cuts - everyone earning over $100 a month had to accept a 10 per cent cut. The founders cut their own substantial salaries in half.

So it was hardly surprising that the 61E never made its projected 1934 launch date. But there were other reasons. It was partly down to indecision over a new OHV 500cc single. Engineering work was done, the Board vacillated, but no firm decision was taken as to which bike to launch first. Then there were problems with the early 61E prototypes. The first engine was complete and in a frame by May 1934, but it immediately showed serious oil leaks from the top-end. Part of this was due to the large number of joints in the new arrangement, but also because there was no attempt to enclose the valve stems or springs. The engineering department argued for a pilot production of 200 bikes to test the water before the main launch, and there were even suggestions at Board level that the whole project be cancelled.

In the event, they compromised. The official launch in 1936 was a low-key affair, and Harley-Davidson stressed to dealers that the new bike was for limited sales only. None of this did any good. There was tremendous interest in the 61E among both dealers and customers. Its existence had been rumoured for some time, and it was the first all-new Harley for a long time. After all, the 61 cu inch capacity was about all it shared with earlier bikes. It had a bigger bore and shorter stroke than the old

61-inch, so it revved harder and produced more power - 4,800rpm and 40bhp from the high compression EL. A proper hemispherical combustion chamber, with 90 degrees between the valves, helped the deep breathing. This was a new breed of Harley-Davidson V-twin, one with plentiful top-end power as well as low- and middle-range pull. Lubrication was markedly different - not total loss, but a modern dry sump recirculating system.

Unfortunately, Harley had failed to get the hang of dry sump design, resulting in some

ABOVE
The Knucklehead brought new style to Harley-Davidson, and this 1939 EL Sports Solo is a prime example

parts of the valve gear being starved of oil while others got too much. It exacerbated the top-end leaks. It must have seemed a very familiar story to Harley-Davidson dealers, who soon received a kit of parts to rectify any oily OHVs. In fact, lubrication was only part of the new bike's problems - valve springs broke (and continued to do so until a new supplier was found) and the timing slipped. The engine's all-iron construction tended to overheat if pushed, and oil consumption was often high. As so often before, Harley had allowed itself to launch a bike that was just not ready, and nearly 100 changes had to be made in the first year.

Yet in that first year, Harley sold nearly 1,900 61Es - it was a success. People took to the bike, not just because of its fast, state-of-the-art engine and new four-speed gearbox. It looked good too. Several Harley-Davidson hallmarks appeared with the 61E, such as the teardrop tank with its built-in speedometer. And there was the apparently minor point that all the mechanical bits neatly filled the spaces within the frame - the cylinders reached right up to the tank, and the new wrap-round oil tank filled the gap behind the engine. Most distinctive, perhaps, were the rocker covers. Some people fancied the big rocker-arm nuts made the covers look like knuckles - hence 'Knucklehead'. So well-received was the Knucklehead's styling, that in 1937 the look was transferred to all the Harley twins, even the workaday 45.

Despite the new bike's success, the founders naturally wanted to prove that its early problems had been overcome. So

Knucklehead 61E

SPECIFICATION

Engine	45-degree V-twin, air-cooled, overhead valve
Bore x stroke	3 $5/16$ x 3 $1/2$in
Capacity	60.33ci (989cc)
Compression ratio	Solo: E - 6.5:1
	EL - 7:1
	Sidecar: E - 5.5:1
	EL - 6:1
Carburettor	Linkert 1 $1/4$in
Lubrication	Recirculation by mechanical pump
Power	E - 37bhp @ 4,800rpm
	EL - 40bhp @ 4,800rpm
Gearbox	Four-speed, constant mesh
Drive	Primary - chain
	Final - chain
Clutch	Dry, multiplate
Suspension	Front - Leading link tubular forks
	Rear - None
Wheelbase	59 $1/2$in
Wheels & tyres	4 $1/2$ x 18in
Weight (depending on spec)	515-565lb
Seat height	26in
Fuel consumption	35-50mpg
Top speed	E - 85-90mph
	EL - 90-95mph

Joe Petrali, who by now was acting as mechanic, designer, rider and race manager for the company, helped tune up a 61E and took it to Daytona. The modifications were not extensive - twin carburettors, higher compression, higher lift for the cams and gearing for the transmission. There was also some impressive-looking streamlining, though after this caused near catastrophe at 100mph, Joe ordered its removal. With the high 3:1 top gear, the machine had a theoretical top speed of 160mph, and Walter Davidson promised Joe a $1,000 bonus if he could reach 150! In the event, Joe managed 136.18mph, sufficient to capture the measured mile record, but not enough to get his bonus. Walter Davidson was a hard man.

The Knucklehead's success really marked Harley's final victory over Indian, whose new four cylinder bike had proved a mechanical disaster. For once, Harley had overtaken its arch-rival which had no overhead valve engine to touch the 61E. It mattered little that the Knucklehead cost more than both Harley and Indian's 74 cu inch side-valve V-twins. It was faster than both and looked better, which counted for much. Little wonder that by the late 1930s, two-thirds of bikes registered in the United States were Harley-Davidsons.

Although it was being kept busy by the demands of its new infant, Harley-Davidson did not neglect the rest of the range. In 1937, the V range became the U, which basically involved the adoption of Knucklehead frame, styling and dry sump lubrication. That frame, now used for all twins except the 45, was remarkable for its twin front down-tubes and double-skinned tubing throughout. As well as the frame, the bigger twins also adopted the 61E's lovely streamlined instrument panel, which incorporated ammeter, oil-pressure indicator and ignition switch.

With the 61 cu inch bike now assuming the role of sportster (with a small 's' at this stage) the side-valvers were able to capitalize on their strengths. They were heavy, solid, reliable tourers of around 600lb, but they could cruise all day at 60mph. But try to keep up higher speeds, and the old problem of overheating re-appeared. However, it was not for this reason that customers bought them. The biggest side-valve did not survive the war, though the 74 was allowed to struggle on for another couple of years, to special order. Their place was largely taken by a 74 cu inch version of the 61E, the FL, which appeared in 1941.

While Harley-Davidson was announcing its changes for 1940 - redesigned clutch, aluminium heads, constant mesh gearboxes - Hitler's armies were overrunning Europe. But even by this stage, both Harley-Davidson and Indian had received contracts from Allied and American armies. Every dog has its day and Harley's rugged 45 was certainly coming into its own. What had been an unloved gap-filler in peacetime had its finest hour in time of war. Of the 88,000 bikes which made up Harley-Davidson's wartime production, the vast majority were 45s. And although given its own tag of WLA, the smallest V-twin remained little changed in its wartime guise.

The engine was, of course, in low compression form, had

LEFT
Knucklehead 1939 EL Sports Solo

RIGHT
This WLA has been fully restored and equipped

UH/ULH V-twins

SPECIFICATION

Engine	Air-cooled, side-valve 45-degree V-twin
Bore x stroke	3.422 x 4.25in
Capacity	80ci (1,340cc)
Carburettor	Linkert 1 1/8in
Lubrication	Throttle controlled oil pump, with automatic primary chain oiling
Compression ratio	UH - 5.2:1 ULH - 5.7:1
Power	UH - 38.5bhp @ 4,000rpm ULH - 39bhp @ 4,000rpm
Ignition	Harley-Davidson battery and coil
Gearbox	Three-speed sliding gear. Reverse or four-speed optional
Drive	Primary - chain Final - chain
Clutch	Dry, multiplate
Frame	Tubular steel cradle, twin downtubes
Wheelbase	60in
Wheels	Quickly detachable, interchangeable
Tyres	4.00 x 18in (4.00 x 19in optional)
Suspension	Front - Leading link forks Rear - None
Weight	c 600lb
Seat height	29 ½in
Fuel capacity	c 3 gallons
Oil capacity	8 ¾ pints

enlarged cylinder head finning to aid cooling and a bigger air cleaner. There was a skidplate under the crankcase, a more substantial luggage rack (one of the U.S. requirements was to carry a 40lb radio), black-out lights and a scabbard for machine gun and rifle. Apart from a metal plate carrying oil, spark plug and speed recommendations, that was it. Never a sparkling performer in civilian dress, the WLA could barely scrape 50mph. But unless you were being chased by BMW-mounted Germans, this scarcely mattered. It speaks volumes for the 45's basic ruggedness that in its new, barely changed form, it acquired a reputation for absolute reliability. And this despite little

maintenance and a good deal of misuse. It was standard practice, if the enemy were sighted, to leap out of the saddle leaving the bike to take care of itself.

The early batches of WLAs went, not to the U.S. Army, but to Britain - the Luftwaffe had destroyed Triumph's factory in Coventry. Canada, which entered the war in 1939, also put in substantial orders for 45s, and got its own version of the bike, the WLC. This all meant big changes at Milwaukee, where the company leased extra factory space, hired more workers (Indian tripled its workforce at this time) and introduced new shifts. It is hard to believe that only seven years earlier, there had been Board level talk of closure. For America, the early

years of the war brought economic boom. The trouble was, everyone was working rather then spending, and very few civilian Harley-Davidsons reached the market. There were some 74- and 80-inch side-valves for the police and armed forces, and a batch of 61-inch Knuckleheads went down the line for the Navy. Otherwise, Milwaukee turned out thousands of WLAs.

Some said it was overwork, the sudden demands of maximum production, that caused Walter Davidson's death in February 1942, though he had been suffering from a liver disorder for some time. He had been the company's figurehead almost from the beginning - builder of the first

WLA

SPECIFICATION

Engine	Air-cooled side-valve 45-degree V-twin
Bore x stroke	2 ¾ x 3 ¹³/₁₆in
Capacity	45ci (747cc)
Compression ratio	5:1
Power	23bhp @ 4,600rpm
Torque	28lb ft @ 3,000rpm
Gearbox	Three-speed constant mesh
Gear ratios	First - 11.71:1
	Second - 7.45:1
	Top - 4.74:1
Wheelbase	57 ½in
Tyres	Standard - 4.00 x 18in
	Desert - 5.50 x 16in
Suspension	Front - Leading link forks
	Rear - None
Weight (without armament)	540lb
Seat height	32in
Ground clearance (to skidplate)	4in
Fording depth	18in max.
Fuel	72 octane min.
Fuel consumption	37mpg
Top speed	65mph
Maximum grade ability	30%
Fuel capacity	3 ⅜ gallons
Oil capacity	1 ⅛ gallons
Cruising range (approx)	125 miles

Harley-Davidsons and company President since 1907. He was succeeded in September 1943 by Bill Harley, who had overseen all Harley design from the start. William Davidson had died five years earlier, which just left Arthur, one of the original four founders. He was now 63 and not in the best of health. Fortunately there was no lack of Davidsons and Harleys to take up the reins - William's son William H. Davidson took on the leadership, while the engineering side remained Harley territory. Apart from a brief interlude when long-time employee William Ottaway was Chief Engineer, the mantle was assumed by Bill Harley's son, another William.

The WLA was a great success, but some of the military hierarchy had been very impressed with the way Rommel's BMW flat twin outfits had performed across the North African desert. They determined that the U.S. Army should have something similar and with drive shaft. Both Indian and Harley were instructed to build flat twins. Harley-Davidson speeded its development by somehow managing to procure a BMW from Holland. So the experimental XA was really little more than a copy of the German machine. Like the BMW, it had shaft drive, a side-valve flat twin of 45 cu inches and Harley's first-ever foot gearchange/hand clutch set-up. On the other hand, it apparently also suffered lubrication and valve gear problems, features probably absent in the original.

Still, it was what the Army wanted, and they liked it. With its cylinders sticking out in the breeze, the XA ran cooler than the WLA and could cover 15,000 miles before engine overhauls. It did come more expensive than the faithful V-twin of course, and Harley-Davidson quoted a unit price of $870 for the initial first thousand, or $430 if the proposed order for 25,000 XAs became a reality. In the event, the order was limited to 1,000 - the Jeep had come along and proved itself in many different ways far more suitable than a motorcycle. Harley-Davidson went back to making WLAs.

While the war meant boom production for Harley, it also stimulated a plethora of R & D projects, most of which never saw battle. In overhead valve form, the XA engine almost found home in a generator set, of

FAR LEFT
1943 WLC. You'd never think this was
an ex-army bike

LEFT
Owner John 'Toby' Low made a good job
of disguising his bike's military origins

BELOW
After the war, many ex-army bikes
(some still crated and unused) were
quickly sold off and civilianized, this
one very convincingly

which the Army ordered nearly 5,000. But the war came to an end and everything was cancelled. Then there was the idea for a mini-Jeep, built by Willy's and powered by a fan-cooled XA engine. Four engines were delivered to Willy's, though this too came to nothing. Similarly there was the Canadian mini-tank engine (or it may have been for a remote-controlled minesweeper, depending on who you believe.) The idea for this was two Knuckleheads linked together - but apparently the Canadians lost interest. Then there was the trike saga. The Army did not approve of sidecars, but did find the trike format attractive; a sort of Servi-Car in uniform. Sixteen prototypes were built, some with 61-inch engines, others with special 69-inchers, and all with shaft drive. Alternatively, the Army could have plumped for the XS - an XA-engined sidecar outfit with driven sidecar wheel. Unfortunately, the Jeep was enough to make all these unfeasible.

CHALLENGE AND RESPONSE

In 1945, when G.I.s were starting to return from all over the world, Harley-Davidson seemed set fair for a new period of prosperity. After all, many of these young men had learnt to ride motorcycles during the war and would want one of their own as civilians. Since the Depression, there was a pent-up hunger for consumer goods which the late 1930s recovery had left unsatisfied. Harley's range, meanwhile, was prestigious and well proven: Indian, its only real domestic rival, was a mere shadow of its former self. Harley-Davidson should have taken full advantage of this situation in the two decades following the war.

But this is not quite what happened. Instead, the company was forced to go public in order to raise cash, then submit to a *de facto* takeover. What went wrong?

Central to Harley's early post-war performance were first British, then Japanese imports to which (Sportster excepted) the company mounted no direct challenge. When dealers inquired of the management (and they often did) why there were no light and middleweight Harley-Davidsons, the two-fold answer was always the same. First, there was not enough money to build expensive prototypes; though less attention to dividends and more to investment would have helped. And second, Harley-Davidson insisted they knew what the American motorcyclist wanted - a big V-twin; those little imports were just not right for the American market. To an Englishman, this would sound horribly familiar. The British bike industry was to trot out exactly this same 'We know best' line. And the Japanese took advantage of the situation.

There is some slight mitigation of Harley's attitude in that the true traditionalist would be unlikely ever to consider any other alternative to the Harley-Davidson. But there was also a new breed of motorcyclist for whom 700lb of V-twin was excessive, while a nippy single of half the weight was just right. It would be unfair though, to accuse the company of resting on its wartime laurels - it was spending money on some things. The highspot of the 1947 dealers' convention was the unveiling of Harley-Davidson's latest acquisition - a massive production plant at Wauwatosa, Wisconsin. Shortly to be equipped with new machine tools, it promised a 50 per cent increase in capacity. According to President William H. Davidson, $3.5 million was being spent on the project. Perhaps the money would have been better spent on new models, for the expected upsurge in demand never came.

*   *   *

But to turn back to the immediate post-war period. With the demands of rebuilding shattered economies, materials were scarce, particularly for such frivolities as motorcycles. So Harley was forced to content itself with a re-introduction of the 1941 range virtually unchanged. Limited numbers of 45 and 74 side-valves, and 61 and 74 Knuckleheads began to trickle out of the Juneau Avenue works. But production was soon up to pre-war levels, with over 15,000 bikes produced in 1946, and over 20,000 the year after.

Neither did it take long for the first big changes to manifest themselves. Late 1947 brought hydraulic tappets and aluminium heads to the big V-twins; the Panhead had arrived. Like many previous Harleys, it was claimed the

TOP
Blue-faced speedometer in angular cover came along in 1947

BOTTOM
Spotlight bar and rear carrier are period extras

RIGHT
After the war, the W series 45s continued as a civilian bike - this pleasant powder blue is a 1948 example

changes would cure overheating and lubrication problems. And like many previous Harleys, they were only a partial cure.

Despite uprating, the oil pump was designed to force lubricant up through a cat's cradle of oilways (no external lines on the Panhead). This meant erratic oil pressure, which upset the hydraulic tappets, which in turn altered the valve timing and could snap rocker-arms. In what had become a familiar ritual, a cure was hastily devised and kits of parts sent out to the dealers. These dealers must have had a highly developed sense of *déja vu* by now. A more permanent improvement came later, when the hydraulic tappets were moved from the top to the base of the pushrods - at least now if oil pressure did vary, it would not affect the timing so much.

There was one other aspect of the Panhead's lube system which caused the odd problem. The design department had hit on the idea of improving rocker arm oiling by sticking a felt pad to the underside of each rockerbox. In theory, this would catch oil splashes and then drip them on to the rockers. Inevitably, there were Sunday-morning mechanics who thought the felt was a factory mistake and removed it. The resulting clatter from the top-end was not due to insufficient lubrication - the felt pads helped damp out resonance in the big pan-shaped rocker covers.

These early problems should not, however, detract too much from the Panhead's success. Like every other Harley which suffered teething problems (and there were plenty of these) it soon settled down into a thoroughly dependable piece of machinery. Moreover, the alloy heads were a genuine step forward, giving better cooling

and less weight. But the real point was that, having got the engine sorted out, Harley-Davidson could almost forget about it and concentrate on bringing the running gear up to date. And apart from the odd power increase, that is exactly what they did over the next 18 years.

First came telescopic front forks in 1949 - Harley's 40-year love affair with leading links was over. The benefits of oil damped forks, with their greatly increased travel, were abundantly clear to anyone brought up on the almost rigid leading links. For most, the vast increase in comfort was well worth the slight trade-off in low speed handling precision. And those forks, standard on both the 61 and 74 cu inch Panheads, brought with them a new name - Hydra-Glide. The year 1952 saw another break with tradition. The hand gearchange and foot clutch arrangement was at last dumped in favour of the now standard foot gearchange and handlebar clutch lever. Traditionalists could still have the old system if they insisted, but times were changing.

Harley-Davidson was not completely deaf to demands for a lightweight bike, but neither was it inclined to fork out for the R & D to build one. A solution presented itself in the form of a little German two-stroke. It was really a DKW, a ready-made 125 offered to Allied bikemakers as post-war reparations. BSA took it on and named it the Bantam; Harley did the same and came up with the Hummer.

FAR LEFT TOP
The bike is standard apart from Panhead telescopic forks, a common mod. They have rake adjustment to facilitate the use of a sidecar

FAR LEFT BELOW
Minimalist instrument panel is a Harley trademark, as on this 1950 Panhead

TOP
Sometimes an old motorcycle is irresistible to passersby with a camera

BOTTOM LEFT
This is a bike with a history, reputedly part of the Bolivian Presidential Guard. One of the last side-valve big twins to leave the factory, it was built in 1946, in the shadow of re-emerging Knuckleheads

BOTTOM RIGHT
Hand gearchange/foot clutch was still the standard set-up when this Harley was made

Panhead FL

SPECIFICATION

Engine	Air-cooled, 45-degree V-twin, overhead valves, hydraulic tappets
Cylinder heads	Aluminium alloy, with aluminium-bronze valve seats and steel valve guides
Cylinder barrels	Cast iron
Bore x stroke	3 $^7/_{16}$ x 3 $^{31}/_{32}$in
Capacity	74ci (1200cc)
Carburettor	Schebler 1 $^5/_{16}$in
Lubrication	Dry sump
Power	c 45bhp @ 4,800rpm
Gearbox	Four-speed constant mesh
Drive	Primary - chain
	Final - chain
Clutch	Dry, multiplate
Suspension	Front - Hydra-Glide hydraulic forks
	Rear - None
Frame	Tubular steel cradle, twin loop
Wheelbase	59 $^1/_2$in
Wheels & tyres	5.00 x 16in
Brakes	Front - 8in drum
	Rear - 8in drum
Weight	560lb
Fuel capacity	3 $^3/_4$ gallons
Oil capacity	1 gallon

The emphasis was on simplicity. Appearing in 1947, the Hummer (it was actually called the S-125 at first) boasted 3bhp from its two-stroke engine, rubber-band front suspension and a rigid rear. It had only three speeds and was given relatively large 3.25 section tyres to soften the ride. It was light, of course, about three Hummers were equal in weight to a Panhead. And on a good day it could creep over 50mph, which made it faster than a WLA.

There was plenty of competition though. The 125 utility market was just starting to expand in the United States, and various Villiers-powered British bikes (James, Francis-Barnett, Royal Enfield) were out there and selling. Of course, Harley-Davidson had a big advantage over all of them - its massive dealer network. So it was a pity that some Harley dealers apparently refused to have anything to do with the Hummer. After a generation of selling big V-twins, the little Hummer was too much of a culture shock for them.

Luckily, not all dealers were so short-sighted, and around 10,000 Hummers were sold in the first year. Unlike the European commuter market, 125s in the United States went mainly to newsboys and kids, and the advertizing reflected that. The same was true of colour schemes, and Hummers often left the factory in bright reds, yellows and blues - it was so different to anything else that had come out of Milwaukee. It sold well enough to boost Harley production to 31,000 in 1948, a figure which seemed to suggest that the post-war recovery was complete.

This success was short-lived. As was the case with BSA's Bantam, Harley-Davidson tended to neglect its little 125. It did get miniaturized teleglide forks in 1951 and a couple of capacity increases, first to 165cc, then 175, but that was about it. Consequently, sales fell off, and the Hummer never managed again to equal the success of that first year. In 1956, a little over 2,000 were made. However, the 165cc engine also found a home in the Topper scooter. Comparison could be made with BSA-Triumph, for like Harley-Davidson, the Brits entered the scooter market late and never managed to equal the zip and style of the Italian originals. Despite this, Harley-Davidson's Topper lasted five years (1960-65), was available in 5 or 9bhp versions and had fully-automatic transmission. Starting was by recoil, rather like a lawnmower. What must the redneck dealers

1947 S-125

SPECIFICATION

Engine	Air-cooled, single cylinder two-stroke
Bore x stroke	2 1/16 x 2 9/32in (52.4 x 57.9mm)
Capacity	7.6ci (124.9cc)
Compression ratio	6.6:1
Power	3bhp
Lubrication	Total loss
Drive	Primary - chain
	Final - chain
Gearbox	Three-speed, unit construction
Gear ratios	First - 29.3:1
	Second - 15.4:1
	Top - 8.45:1
Tyres	3.25 x 19in
Wheelbase	50in
Weight	175lb
Fuel capacity	1 3/4 gallons
Gearbox oil	1 1/4 pints

FAR LEFT
Ken Lee's Topper is one of only eight imported into Europe, and it's probably the only one still running

BOTTOM
Petroil lubrication for the 6bhp two-stroke single, but the really interesting bit is that grey wheel behind it. It's one of the expanding pulleys which changed size (and thus ratio) as engine and rider demanded

LEFT
The Topper's square-rigged appearance betrayed its genuine Milwaukee origins. Would Vespa have ever come up with something so totally lacking in style?

have thought?

The Hummer was all very well, but hardly the bike to encourage young riders to graduate to a V-twin. Neither was it the bike to challenge the new wave of British exports. At first it was 350 singles, then 500s; then 500 twins, then 650s. About 9,000 such bikes were imported in 1946, and 15,000 the following year. Of course,

they were not perfect - the oil leaks rivalled anything a Harley could produce and they lacked the staying power for long, hot, American highways. On the other hand, they were light, flickable, and fast - a revelation to anyone brought up on 600lb V-twins. And Harley had nothing to rival them, not a thing.

The answer came in the form

of Harley's 'baby' V-twin, the 45-inch side-valve - now known as the WL. This, to put it mildly, was a joke. In spite of an engine massively larger than any of the imports, the WL could barely hit 70mph when most of the foreign 500s could top 90mph. It weighed about 150lb more, and was still stuck with a hand gearchange.

There was a suggestion in the late '40s that Harley-Davidson might try to meet the imports head on. A proposal to the Board suggested a shaft drive vertical twin, with hydraulic forks, rear suspension and foot gearchange. All this came to nothing, and the experience of Indian may have had something to do with it. Long ago relegated to an also-ran in the U.S. bike industry, Indian threw itself wholeheartedly into meeting the foreign challenge, and designed middleweight vertical twins called Arrow and Scout. Unfortunately, the new bikes turned out to be fragile in the extreme, resulting in massive warranty claims which undoubtedly encouraged Indian's downfall.

Whether influenced by the Indian experience or not, Harley-Davidson decided upon another tack. It presented a submission in 1950 to the U.S. Tariff Commission in which it sought to increase import duty on foreign bikes which had by then captured 40 per cent of the market. When this failed (partly due to damning evidence of Harley's less then liberal attitude towards its dealers) the company bowed to the inevitable. It would have to produce a serious competitor.

*　　*　　*

At first sight, the new K model looked as though it had all the right ingredients. Modern styling (streets ahead of the W with its roots in the 1920s), unit construction, suspension at *both ends*, foot gearchange, clutch on the handlebar - the K looked just the thing to fight the imports. But there was a fatal flaw. It had side-valves. Why did Harley, who had been selling OHVs for 16 years, go for a flathead when everything else on the new bike was bang up-to-date?

Maybe Harley-Davidson was trying to please too many people at once - sleek styling for the young, side-valves to reassure the traditionalists. Or maybe so much time had been devoted to developing the chassis that there was not enough left over for the

RIGHT
The 45in side-valve is not everyone's first choice for customizing, but it is different

K model

SPECIFICATION	
Engine	Air-cooled 45-degree V-twin, side-valves
Cylinder heads	Light alloy
Cylinder barrels	Cast iron
Bore x stroke	2 ¾ x 3 ¹³/₁₆in
Capacity	45ci (747cc)
Power	c 30bhp
Lubrication	Recirculation, with gear-type pressure and scavenge pumps. Separate supplies for primary chain and gearbox
Carburettor	Linkert
Drive	Primary - triplex chain Final - chain
Clutch	Dry, multiplate
Gearbox	Four-speed constant-mesh, unit construction
Brakes	Front - 8in drum Rear - 8in drum
Tyres	3.25 x 19in
Suspension	Front - telescopic forks with hydraulic damping Rear - swinging arm with coil springs and hydraulic damping
Frame	Tubular steel cradle, twin loop
Fuel capacity	4 ½ gallons
Oil capacity	6 pints

OVERLEAF MAIN PICTURE
Big bike, satisfied owner

INSET OVERLEAF LEFT
Like most of the big twins, the Panhead evolved into a reliable unit, after the customary Harley-Davidson teething problems

INSET OVERLEAF RIGHT
Saddlebags are another typical extra of the time, though the silencer is a little more recent

engine. Then there is the stop-gap argument. According to William H. Davidson, the K was just a gap-filler, something to sell against Triumph while Harley-Davidson designed its real Thunderbird rival. On the other hand, it was to be another five years before that bike (the XL) appeared, which seems to make nonsense of the stop-gap theory.

The engine was not a straight carry-over from the W series, though just how new it was depends on which Harley historian you believe. It was either 'of the 1920 era' (Harry Sucher), a 'revamped' version of the W (David Wright) or 'all-new' (Thomas Bolfert). Certainly the crankcases were new for unit construction, and if bore, stroke and capacity were

identical to the old, then the light alloy heads were a genuine advance. Unfortunately, 30bhp was still not enough to impress Triumph riders. The standard K struggled to better 80mph, and apparently had little acceleration above 60. To add insult to injury, the racing KR version made less power than the old WR.

Harley's answer was two-fold. In 1954, the capacity was upped to 55 cu inches (which helped a bit but not enough) and there were hotter versions, the 45-inch KK and 55-inch KHK which used the racer's cams and valves. They were by all accounts a great improvement but there was still no reflection in sales, and in 1956 Harley sold only a little over 1,200 K bikes. To put that in a wider context, it

also sold over 2,200 Hummers and over 5,700 big twins that year. And, inevitably, certain problems developed which had somehow failed to show up on the prototypes. The most serious was gear-teeth breakage, later solved by the use of forged gears. Still, the engine proved mercifully free of trouble, so perhaps there was something to be said for Harley-Davidson's conservative streak after all. Anyway, in 1957 came the bike the K should have been in the first place - the Sportster.

Some people believe the Honda 750 to be the first ever superbike. Others would plump for the early ZI Kawasaki. Others still favour one of the British contenders - V-twins from Brough Superior and Vincent, or the BSA/Triumph triples. But for

Harley-lovers there can only be one - the XLCH Sportster. The XL's significance was not that it was faster than anything else - it was soon overtaken in the outright horsepower race - but it marked Harley-Davidson's return as a maker of serious performance motorcycles.

With the Sportster, they got it right first time. It looked right too; slim and stripped in a way that standard Harleys had not looked for years. It retained all the good features of the KH and added overhead valves, more revs and a lot more power. The secret lay in not having the valves on top, but in the heart of the engine. Although identical in capacity to the KH, the Sportster used the 45-inch K's shorter stroke with a bigger three-inch bore. The result was still well undersquare, but that relatively short stroke allowed higher revs (by Harley-Davidson standards) and the big bore could accomodate big valves. The result was 40bhp at 5,500rpm - at last, a Harley that could outrun Triumph - on the straight at least. It was still heavier and less flickable than a Thunderbird, but here was a genuine 100mph road bike, with acceleration to match.

Otherwise, little was changed from the old KH - the same unit construction four-speed gearbox (though now with removable cover to aid servicing); same frame, suspension and brakes. Despite appearances, the engine was in a fairly low state of tune at first, with a compression ratio of only 7.5:1. Things changed within a year though. February 1958 brought the XLH, with its 9:1 ratio (thanks to domed pistons), smoothed up ports, larger valves and aluminium tappets. But despite all the performance, Harley-Davidson still seemed a little unsure of its bike's real purpose. It still had the big four-gallon tank as

1957 XL/1969 XLCH

SPECIFICATION

Engine	Air-cooled 45-degree V-twin, OHV
Bore x stroke	3 x 3 $^{13}/_{16}$in
Capacity	53.9ci (883cc)
Compression ratio	XL - 7.5:1
	XLCH - 9:1
Power	XL - 40bhp @ 5,500rpm
	XLCH - 55bhp @ 6,800rpm
Carburettor	XL - Linkert
	XLCH - Tillotson 1.62in
Lubrication	Dry sump, with gear-type pump
Ignition	XL - Battery and coil
	XLCH - Magneto (coil on later models)
Drive	Primary - triplex chain
	Final - chain
Clutch	Dry, multiplate
Gearbox	Four-speed constant-mesh, unit construction
Gear ratios (XLCH)	1st - 11.74:1
	2nd - 8.50:1
	3rd - 6.43:1
	4th - 4.66:1
Suspension	Front - Telescopic fork with hydraulic damping
	Rear - Swinging arm with hydraulic dampers
Brakes	XL: Front - 8 x 1in drum
	Rear - 8 x 1in drum
	XLCH: Front - 8 x 1 $^{1}/_{2}$in drum
	Rear - 8 x 1in drum
Tyres	XL - 3.50 x 18in
	XLCH: Front - 3.75 x 19in
	Rear - 4.25 x 18in
Weight	c 500lb
Seat height (XLCH)	30 $^{1}/_{2}$in
Fuel capacity	XL - 4.4 gallons
	XLCH - 2.25 gallons
Oil capacity	6 pints

Performance:
(XLCH tested by *Cycle World* Nov 1969)

Top speed	112.48mph
Speeds in gears	1st - 44mph
	2nd - 61mph
	3rd - 81mph
0-60mph	4.9 secs
Standing quarter	14.25 sec/95.03mph
Fuel consumption	39mpg

standard, and all the usual touring gear (luggage racks, panniers, screens) was optional. So you could, if you liked, turn your XL into a mini-Panhead. What a waste!

But there were several Harley-Davidson dealers with no such schizophrenia and Harley at last started to listen to its long-suffering salesforce. They wanted a stripped down XL to sell - and in 1959 they got it. According to Allan Girdler, there were actually a few hundred stripped-down XLCs delivered the previous year, the result of a request from Californian dealers. The bike everyone knows, the XLCH, was a natural progression.

It must be said that the CH was more about style than extra speed. It was no more powerful than the XLH, and the only significant mechanical change was magneto ignition in place of the coil and battery. Though this

was later changed back to coil when starting became too much of a chore for increasingly sophisticated riders. But it was the appearance of the thing that really mattered. Whether by luck or judgement, the use of Hummer's tiny 2.25 gallon tank set the whole thing off to a tee. So much so that the less than useful 80-mile range paled to relative insignificance. Skimpier mudguards, shorter seat and (to suggest off-roading) high-level pipes and semi-knobbly tyres completed the stripped-down look. Although the advertizements depicted CHs dashing through dirt and leaping logs, most bikes ended up on the street, and this was honestly where this 500lb motorcycle belonged.

Later in 1959 there were higher-lift camshafts, to boost power again to 55bhp - but all XLs got the same power, whether their aspirations were

towards touring or competition. One other thing about the Sportster was that, although rightly acclaimed a classic, its effect on Harley-Davidson's sales was less clear-cut. In 1955, the company produced a low of less then 10,000 bikes. The figure wavered around the 12-15,000 mark in the late '50s, but was down again in the early part of the following decade. The Sportster did wonders for company image but failed to turn Harley round. Until 1965, when the company had just 6 per cent of the market, it never made more than a quarter of total sales. That same year, with money running short again, Harley-Davidson was forced to go public. For the first time, ownership of the company was to pass from family monopoly.

BOTTOM
The tank treatment on this Sportster looks quite understated, until you realize that it is real gold plating

TIDDLERS AND TAKEOVERS

Harley-Davidson appeared to have an aversion to anything other than V-twins. Look at the evidence. Everything else, apart from the first singles, was either heavily influenced by existing designs (Sport Twin, inter-war singles) or was a virtual bolt-for-bolt copy (Hummer). In 1960 Harley took the further step of putting its badge to bikes that were not even built in Milwaukee.

From a pragmatic corporate point of view, there was much to recommend this. In theory, they would gain access to a ready-made range of (hopefully) well-proven light and middleweight bikes. As the 1950s gave way to the '60s,

Harley-Davidson realized that it needed something new - the Hummer was by now old hat, and in any case could not hope to compete with the middleweights. The answer

FAR RIGHT
Aermacchi's simple pushrod engine was remarkably powerful, but torquey too

BELOW
Harley needed an answer to the British and Japanese imports, and this was it, an Italian bike with Harley-Davidson badges. This Sprint is owned by Tracey Lee

seemed to lie in Aermacchi, a company based at Varese, Italy. It had an 80mph 250 single and was in desperate need of capital.

So it was that Harley-Davidson bought 50 per cent of Aermacchi, sent a few representatives over to Varese, and very soon had a market-ready 250 to sell at a competitive price. According to Harry Sucher, the Sprint (as it was marketed in the United States) owed much to the Moto Guzzi Falcone. Hence the four-stroke single cylinder engine, mounted horizontally. With an 8.5:1 compression ratio it gave 18bhp at 7,500rpm. It was, of course, something totally

1968 Sprint SS350

SPECIFICATION

Engine	Air-cooled four-stroke single, OHV
Bore x stroke	2.9 x 3.15in (74 x 80mm)
Capacity	21ci (350cc)
Compression ratio	9:1
Power	25bhp @ 7,000rpm
Carburettor	Dellorto 27mm
Lubrication	Wet sump
Ignition	Battery and coil
Drive	Primary - helical gears
	Final - chain
Clutch	Dry, multiplate
Gearbox	Four-speed constant mesh, unit construction
Gear ratios	1st - 18.18:1
	2nd - 11.00:1
	3rd - 7.95:1
	4th - 6.25:1
Suspension	Front - telescopic fork with hydraulic damping
	Rear - swinging arm with hydraulic damping
Brakes	Front - 7.1 x 1.38in drum
	Rear - 7.1 x 1.38in drum
Tyres	Front - 3.25 x 19in
	Rear - 3.50 x 18in
Weight	323lb
Wheelbase	53.3in
Seat height	30.8in
Fuel capacity	2.65 gallons
Oil capacity	4 pints

Performance:
(SS350 tested by *Cycle World* Nov 1968)

Top speed	92.5mph
Speed in gears	1st - 28.2mph
	2nd - 47.4mph
	3rd - 64.5mph
0-60mph	8.0 secs
Standing quarter	15.85 secs/80.78mph
Fuel consumption	46.1mpg

different for Harley, with its single-strut frame from which the engine was suspended. Harley-Davidson tried to soften its rather different appearance by giving it styling features from the bigger bikes, right down to a big chrome air-cleaner cover.

The Sprints were fast, light, and easy to ride, but were not without problems. The chief ones seem to have been, not the engine, but ancillaries such as electrics. Aermacchi bought in most of the components from outside suppliers, which

provided headaches of a particularly severe kind for the Harley men in Varese, trying their best to track down quality-control problems. And there were inevitable problems of communication between factories thousands of miles apart.

There were, however, some useful advances. A street scrambler version, the Sprint H, appeared in 1962. Higher compression and new carburettor followed in 1964, giving a power boost to 25bhp, and in 1968 the engine became a 350. The Sprint even secured the world 250cc speed record in 1965 - 177mph at the Bonneville flats for a streamliner ridden by George Roeder. But by the late '60s, the Aermacchi, which had seemed so up-to-the-minute at the start of the decade, was looking increasingly old-fashioned next to the Japanese bikes, with their overhead cams and electric starts. In 1973, the Sprint, now sold in SS350 (road) and SX350 (trail) forms, did get an electric foot. But the Japanese bikes were both cheaper and more sophisticated.

Then there were the dealers to contend with. In a repeat of Hummer's fate, some apparently refused to have anything to do with the bike. To them it was a nasty little 'furrin' motorcycle which just did not deserve to have the hallowed Harley badge on its tank. But a glance at the sales figures tells a different story. Only 1,566 Sprints were sold in 1963, but double that in '65. From then onwards, until it was dropped in 1974, a steady 4-6,000 found homes every year. Except 1967, when 9,000 were imported - it outsold the Sportster two to one that year. Perhaps the Sprint's real tragedy was that it introduced thousands of learner riders to Harley-Davidson, yet there was no 500/650 to which they could graduate.

☆   ☆   ☆

So while Harley was inventing the superbike and selling Italian lightweights, what of the Panhead? All through the 1950s and early '60s it soldiered on. For many it was the definitive Harley, a spiritual successor to the Knucklehead, VL, even the earliest V-twins. And it remained the mainstay of the range, outselling everything else by a large margin. Not that it was being ignored; a tougher bottom end came in 1954, which allowed a 12 per cent power jump the following year.

Greater things were achieved in 1958 when the Panhead acquired swinging arm rear suspension and a new name, Duo Glide. It worked well, in a soft, spongy, tourer kind of way. But some traditionalists objected - a big balloon tyre was quite enough rear suspension for them. Anything else was a sop to fickle fashion. Hence the demand for aftermarket hardtail frames. In 1959 there were hydraulic brakes (still drums, of course) but it took another six years for the definitive Panhead to emerge.

It was inevitable that Harley-Davidson would have to fit electric starters. But when it happened it was in typical Harley fashion - the starter motor, bigger battery and 12 volt conversion added a massive 75lb to the Panhead's kerb weight. From all this, despite initial imperfections, the Electra Glide emerged and its name lives on today.

ABOVE
A Harley-Davidson and the Big Sky - what a picture!

LEFT
Whitewalls were standard on the 5.00 x 16in tyres, either Goodyear or Firestone

TOP RIGHT
Owner Smokey did all the work himself - Silver Mist and Regal Blue, with red highlights

BOTTOM RIGHT
Someone with a sense of humour brought this 90cc two-stroke Harley to a HOG rally. Note the classic custom touches!

In the year of the Electra Glide, another new bike went on sale, and they had nothing in common except for the name on the tank. It was the M50, Aermacchi's moped, which the advertizements assured would bring, 'Fun for Young America, at any age.' There was nothing particularly distinguished about the M50 - just another 50cc two-stroke step-through like thousands of others being made in Europe and Japan. Still, according to factory figures, there was an initial surge of interest in the little bike and they produced 9,000 in 1965 and over 16,000 the year after. Then just as suddenly, interest faded. Despite the extra 15cc in 1967 (for which Harley-Davidson claimed an improbable 62 per cent power boost) sales of the new M65 never reached the earlier heights. In Sport form (which had vaguely motorcycle-like styling) it hung on until 1972.

What the M50 did mark was the beginning of a succession of Aermacchi two-strokes. The Rapido, Baja 100 and TX/SX off-road series were not as well-made as the Japanese bikes, and they tended to follow fashion rather than lead it. But the price was right, they looked the part, and sold well.

The Rapido 125 appeared first, in 1968. It was hardly high-tech, you still had to pre-mix the petroil, and there were only four gears to play with. But it was sturdy and reliable, a worthy successor to the old DKW-based Hummer. Three of them were ridden across the Sahara one year, when Russell Rehm, Dick Ewing and Frank Fanger rode from Casablanca to the Dahomey coast. The Rapido's staid styling belied its name, but that was about to change. The Baja 100, in 1970, was the first sign that Harley-Davidson was beginning to regard the little bikes as something more than commuter fodder. It was basically the Rapido's engine sleeved down to 98cc, in an off-road chassis. Intended for competition (lighting was an option) the Baja made a good start, winning its class in the Greenhorn Enduro

one year. Unfortunately, *Cycle World* was less than effusive after a brief test in May 1970. They disliked the 35-inch seat height, high centre of gravity and electrics and brakes which disliked water.

In the meantime, the Rapido had been brought bang up-to-date as the TX125. Trail bike styling, five-speed gearbox and automatic oil injection were just the thing to challenge the Japanese. It was not designed for serious off-roading, but then neither was much of the opposition. Harley sold over 9,000 of them in 1973 and followed up with a 175cc version in '74 and a 250 the year after. There was a bewildering array of model designations - SX, SS, SXT - and just what they all stood for, no one seems to know. The 250 was apparently quite spritely, being a match for anything apart from the purpose-built off-roaders. A pity, then, that *Cycle World's* test bike blew up two gearboxes and the $1130 price tag was considered excessive. Still, 11,000 found buyers in 1975 (though those heights were never achieved again) so some people must have liked them.

But in the end, it was still not enough to keep pace with the Japanese, who dominated the market. After all this time there were still problems with Harley dealers who saw the two-strokers merely as a sideline. Then there was the great American public for whom Harley-Davidson meant V-twin and nothing else. Harley's very strength in one sector, it seemed, was its weakness elsewhere. So the link with Aermacchi was severed, and the Varese plant sold. Since then, Harley has tended to stick to what it knows best.

* * *

We left the Panhead in 1965, with its newly acquired electric

starter. Things were not going well for Harley-Davidson. Despite its virtual monopoly of big tourers, it had just 6 per cent of the total market. Part of the reason was that while the bike market was growing fast (Honda's 'nicest people' campaign was bearing fruit) America's only motorcycle manufacturer was stagnating. There had been only incremental changes to the Panhead, while the Sportster, such a big step in the right direction when it came out, was being seemingly neglected. Then there were the production facilities - certainly large, but

seriously outdated. Meanwhile, those British bikes, the 500 twins, had grown into 650s and 750s - more serious head-on competition for the V-twins. Perhaps most serious of all, Harley-Davidson simply did not have the cash to solve any of these problems.

It seems strange that a company which had made consistent profits for years and enjoyed sales of over $30 million should find itself with insufficient capital. But that was the situation, and also the reason why Harley-Davidson had to offer shares for general sale. The

now 60bhp, though the last of the Panheads produced had been just as powerful, uprated to cope with the extra weight of that electric start. There were still FL (low compression) and FLH (high compression) versions. It was even possible to order a hand gearstick.

The Sportster, which had hardly changed in the early '60s, did get better brakes in 1964, 12 volt electrics in '66 and the electric start the year after that. With 58bhp at 6,800rpm, it produced almost as much power as the FLH, and had succeeded in carving out its own style niche. But during this period Harley's sales stayed virtually constant while the market continued to head upwards. The company was running short of money again.

This time, another share issue would not be enough, and the

management was forced to seek a merger. In reality, this meant takeover by some large conglomerate with the money and patience to turn Harley-Davidson around. It was a measure of Harley's standing that two big firms, Bangor Punta and the American Machine and Foundry Company (AMF) were keen to take on the task. AMF emerged the victor, after several months' battle, and took control of Harley-Davidson in January 1969.

LEFT
1967 fully dressed Electra Glide, with only 28,000 miles from new

BOTTOM
The orange bike is really an Aermacchi. With Harley-Davidson cash, the Italians developed a two-stroke 250 twin which could meet and beat the Japanese, at least for a while. Here the legendary Jay Springsteen lines up for a 1978 race at Daytona

reason was simple; Harley had been showing every sign of complacency and poor management.

Financial problems aside, the big V-twin received its second post-war reincarnation in 1966 with the arrival of the Shovelhead. The two new rockerboxes, apparently, looked just like a couple of coal shovels, but little else was actually changed. A few features were adopted from the Sportster and the Shovelhead was genuinely oil tight. But it was still only available as a 74, with separate gearbox. Output was

Much has been written about Harley's AMF period, most of it critical; big, bad, profit-stripping giant exploits poor but honest motorcycle maker - that sort of thing. But it was more complicated than that. By the late '60s, the independent Harley-Davidson was in a mess. Investment had been minimal, the product and factories were outdated and the dealers dispirited. AMF promised, as senior takeover partners invariably do, that nothing would change apart from a fresh injection of capital.

This was nonsense of course. It is quite true that AMF cash was soon being spent on re-equipping the Juneau Avenue and Capitol Drive works, and in 1971 assembly was moved to AMF's existing factory at York. It was long-term investment that Harley-Davidson sorely needed. But to recoup its investment, AMF's reaction was to virtually double the production rate to 50,000 bikes a year. The new frantic pace, coupled with shopfloor resentment at the

imposed changes had the inevitable effect - quality nosedived. For much of the '70s, Harleys were simply badly-built, part-finished bikes. Take the XLCR; the first hundred off the line needed $100,000 of remedial work to make them saleable. At this time, about half the bikes were coming off the line incomplete.

Once again, the long-suffering dealers found themselves in the role of last ditch quality controllers. One hesitates to draw a parallel with the British bike industry, but even as AMF managers were attempting to bring Harley-Davidson into mass production, so an army of accountants were doing the same to BSA-Triumph. In both cases, a great deal of money was invested, though not always in the right places, and grandiose plans made. The difference was that Harley survived while its British rival was destroyed.

There was another difference. At this time Harley-Davidson was in a position to produce new models which were to help

LEFT
Farmer Albert Remme prefers to keep the mileage down and the bike clean; where he lives, there are only dirt roads

TOP
Electra Glide with lots of chrome and whitework, a distinct branch of customizing from the usual lurid murals

see it through a difficult decade. In 1970, the KR racer (still based on the old 45 side-valver) was finally replaced by the XR750. It was really a sized-down 883cc Sportster engine, though it did acquire alloy barrels in 1972. True to form, Harley-Davidson managed to persuade the AMA to change the rules in favour of the new bike, and it

subsequently dominated half mile, mile and TT courses well into the '80s. The other new bike was associated with another area of motorcycle culture, which for Harley-Davidson was to prove even more significant.

People had been chopping Harleys for years, yet the factory had always remained slightly

aloof. The new 1970 Super Glide was really the first official recognition of the way thousands of people wanted their bikes to look. Just as important, it was the first attempt at a factory custom, and Harley-Davidson has been doing well out of the practice ever since. Mechanically, there was nothing new about the

Super Glide with its mating of the FL 1200cc engine and main frame to the Sportster front end. More important was its styling, mainly the work of Willie G. Davidson (son of William H.) The Super Glide had a long, low, stripped-down look, without a hint of either dresser or Sportster about it. And therein lies its true significance. Until now, the Harley-Davidson range was pretty simple - tourers (and more recently) Sportsters. But the Super Glide showed what could be done by a judicious swapping of parts and a few new pieces of glass fibre. Since then, Harley's range has blossomed into a plethora of models, and it is serving them well.

Meanwhile, in 1972, the Sportster was getting its first big change, a new frame and engine bored out to 997cc. The 61-incher was back! Power was up only slightly to 61bhp,

though at a more relaxed 6,200rpm. According to *Cycle World* the new XLCH 1000 was only 4mph faster than the old one and actually slower accelerating up to sixty. It did knock almost a second off the quarter mile time though.

But with its larger engine, the Sportster seemed to be slipping back into the role of mini-FLH. There was a need for some more direct competition for the imports, something more overtly sporting. The result was the XLCR, the boldest statement yet from the styling department. Just like the Super Glide, it was a concoction of various components from the Harley parts bin, backed up with lots of matt black and a single seat. Although dubbed 'Cafe Racer' by the factory, it was a pretty mild one, without the extreme clip-ons and rear sets fitted to the genuine article. The front end and one litre engine were

pure Sportster and the rest of the frame was based on the XR750. But what was fine for a 750cc racer was just not strong enough for a big torquey road bike - there was at least one instance of the frame cracking at

a low mileage. Worse still, the public did not flock to buy the XLCR. Some said it resembled a Jap bike - the XLCR, mild by real cafe racer standards, was just a bit too radical for Harley-Davidson afficionados.

That Willie G.'s third factory custom was a raging success where the XLCR had failed said a lot about Harley and the fact that they now knew what was expected of them. The 1977 FXS Lowrider was no more than a restyled Super Glide, with low seat, flat bars and Fat Bob tank for that ground-hugging look. In short, it was another Harley-Davidson interpretation of what customizers had been doing for years, and the punters loved it. Nearly 10,000 were made in 1978, compared to just 1,201 XLCRs. Underneath it all, the FXS was no different to any other Harley V-twin - big torquey pushrod engine going *chugga-chugga, chugga-chugga*; clonky but strong gearbox; heavy but bullet-proof clutch. It was all very familiar, and that was really what people wanted from Harley-Davidson.

1972 Super Glide

SPECIFICATION

Engine	Air-cooled 45-degree V-twin, OHV
Bore x stroke	87.3 x 100.8mm
Capacity	74ci (1207cc)
Compression ratio	8:1
Power	65bhp @ 5,200rpm
Carburettor	Bendix/Zenith 1 5/8in
Lubrication	Dry sump, gear-type pump
Ignition	Coil and battery
Drive	Primary - duplex chain
	Final - single-row chain
Clutch	Dry, multiplate
Gearbox	Four-speed constant mesh
Gear ratios	1st - 10.74:1
	2nd- 6.50:1
	3rd - 4.39:1
	4th- 3.57:1
Suspension	Front - Telescopic fork with hydraulic damping
	Rear - swinging arm with hydraulic damping
Brakes	Front - 8 x 1.5in drum
	Rear - 8 x 1.825in drum
Tyres	Front - 3.75 x 19in
	Rear - 5.10 x 16in
Weight	559lb
Wheelbase	62.3in
Seat height	28.7in
Fuel capacity	3.5 gallons
Oil capacity	1 gallon

Performance:
(Super Glide tested by *Cycle World* July 1972)

Top speed	108.4mph
Speeds in gears	
(5,500rpm)	1st - 38mph
	2nd - 63mph
	3rd - 93mph
0-60mph	5.6 secs
Standing quarter	14.43 secs/76.33mph
Fuel consumption	47mpg

FAR LEFT TOP
Screen and stylish horn mark out Barry's FLH from all the others. He also made up a rear light bar himself and fitted 1 1/2in longer rear shocks

LEFT
For anyone who thought there was no scope for customizing number plates...

FAR LEFT BOTTOM
Barry Rhodes reckons his '81 FLH is 'a real motorbike', but has no illusions about comfort: 'All this stuff about sitting in an armchair is guff!'

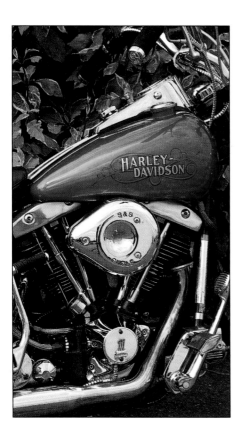

By the late 1970s, the company had left many of its problems behind. Production, after the AMF-inspired height of 75,000 in 1975 had settled back down to a steady, achievable 45-50,000. Quality was back up to scratch and the factory custom strategy was working well. That is not to say that it was under no pressure at all. In 1978 the company tried again to get increased import duties slapped on the competition. Just as in 1951, the idea was thrown out by the Tariff Commission.

There came some useful upgrades to the bikes - the big FL series (now mainly overshadowed by the FX and Sportster) received a capacity boost to 1340cc - or in other words, 80 cu inches. Harley seems to have an obsession with certain engine sizes. Within a couple of years the new 80 incher was the standard engine among FLs. But if order had returned to the factory, the owners were less than happy.

1977 XLCR 1000

SPECIFICATION

Engine	Air-cooled 45-degree V-twin, OHV
Bore x stroke	81 x 97mm
Capacity	60.9ci (997cc)
Compression ratio	9:1
Power	68bhp @ 6,200rpm
Carburettor	Keihin 38mm
Lubrication	Dry sump, gear-type pump
Ignition	Battery and coil
Drive	Primary - triplex chain
	Final - chain
Clutch	Wet, multiplate
Gearbox	Four-speed constant mesh, unit construction
Gear ratios	1st - 11.16:1
	2nd - 8.09:1
	3rd - 6.11:1
	4th - 4.43:1
Suspension	Front - Telescopic forks with hydraulic damping
	Rear - Swinging arm with hydraulic damping
Brakes	Front - Twin discs, 9.88in dia
	Rear - Disc, 9.75in dia
Tyres	Front - MJ90-19
	Rear - MN90-18
Weight	515lb
Wheelbase	58.5in
Seat height	31in
Fuel capacity	4 gallons
Oil capacity	7 ½ pints

Performance:
(XLCR tested by *Cycle World* May 1977)

Top speed	106mph
Speeds in gears	1st - 46mph
	2nd - 63mph
	3rd - 83mph
Standing quarter	13.1 secs/99.7mph
Fuel consumption	43.8mpg

TOP LEFT
Ken Goldsbury's 'Barbarian' is based on a 1972 Shovelhead. Mrs Goldsbury sits at the controls

BOTTOM LEFT
Resplendent Shovelhead Low Rider. Apart from the paintwork, how many other subtle custom add-ons can you see?

TOP RIGHT
The Shovelhead lasted nearly 20 years, the last iron-barrelled Harley engine of the old school

BACK TO THE FUTURE

1980 was a year of change. Not only did belt drive and five-speed gearbox arrive, but the company underwent its second change of ownership in 11 years.

AMF could look back on an expensive decade with Harley-Davidson. A lot of money had been invested, production had been raised, and Harley was in far better competitive shape. But for all its pains, AMF was being told that no good bikes had been made since it took over. The motorcycle industry, as AMF now knew, was not only seasonal, but subject to dramatic peaks and troughs; there was intense (cheaper) competition from Japan. Finally, Harley-Davidson, despite all the investment, was still only making small profits. AMF, as

our American friends would say, wanted out. Negotiations dragged on throughout 1980 and the first half of 1981 until in June it was official. Harley-Davidson was being re-acquired by the buy-back team, a group of top level management who were able to raise money both personally and on the stock market. Harley was independent again, and it has stayed that way ever since.

Even while all this was going on, some important new bikes were appearing. In a break with tradition, the 1980 Tour Glide included not one, but several innovations. There was a new frame, welded rather than cast, and rubber mounting for the engine - at last, an official recognition that Harleys vibrated - it was actually adjustable, like

a Norton Commando. More important, it worked, and *Cycle World* were moved to say that the bike vibrated no more than a steam ship. A five-speed gearbox was fitted as standard (which rapidly permeated across the range) and the front forks were mounted behind the steering head and slightly offset. It set a new standard of manoeuvrability for a big Harley. The chain got full enclosure and an oil bath, but this was just a stopgap.

This became clear later in the year when the Sturgis appeared. Nothing was new about this Lowrider-based bike except for the belt drives. For the first time, perhaps even for the first time ever, Harley-Davidson was first in the market with a new feature. Kawasaki was already

using a final drive belt, but Harley was the first to have a primary belt as well. The technology was actually well established - belts had become commonplace as camshaft drives in cars - and like the rubber mountings, they worked first time out. The toothed rubber belts did need to be aligned properly, but other than that they needed no lubrication or tensioning, and would last for 20,000 miles. Like the five-speed, the belts made their way across the whole range, to the point where they have become a Harley-Davidson trademark.

After all that feverish activity, not much happened in the early '80s, though Harley-Davidson did finally succeed in wresting some import controls out of the Tariff Commission. Restricted to 700cc plus bikes only, it imposed a five year sliding scale of duties starting in 1982. That the company was able to request the ending of duty ahead of schedule is an indication of its continued recovery. For Harley-Davidson was entering a particularly happy period. It seemed to have acknowledged that its bikes were less then perfect, listened to the customers, and acted accordingly.

Two different Sportsters from 1983 illustrate the point. The all-black XLX was a return to the Sportster's roots. All superfluous

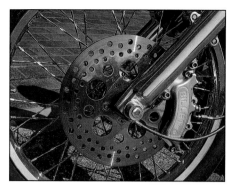

FAR LEFT
Mick Wright's '81 Sturgis had been stolen and recovered only a month before this picture was taken, and it still looks immaculate

BELOW
That brake caliper doesn't look quite muscular enough to stop a 600lb motorcycle in a hurry, one reason why multi-piston Billet set-ups are popular

LEFT
A good shot of a disk brake by Billet

1980 Sturgis FXB-80

SPECIFICATION

Engine	Air-cooled, 45-degree V-twin, OHV
Bore x stroke	88.8 x 107.9mm
Capacity	1340cc
Compression ratio	8:1
Power	Not quoted
Torque	71.5lb ft @ 3,800rpm
Carburettor	Keihin 38mm
Lubrication	Dry sump, gear-type pump
Ignition	Electronic, breakerless
Drive	Primary - Toothed belt (1.125in)
	Final - Toothed belt (1.5in)
Clutch	Dry, multiplate
Gearbox	Four-speed constant mesh
Gear ratios	1st - 8.00:1
	2nd - 5.42:1
	3rd - 4.02:1
	4th - 3.27:1
Suspension	Front - Telescopic forks, 6.9in travel
	Rear - Swinging arm, 3.5in travel
Brakes	Front - Twin discs, 10.0in dia
	Rear - Disc, 10.0in dia
Tyres	Front - MT90-19
	Rear - MT90-16
Weight	610lb
Wheelbase	64.7in
Seat height	27in
Fuel capacity	3 ½ gallons
Oil capacity	4 ½ quarts

Performance:
(FXB tested by *Cycle World* Sept 1980)

Top speed	106mph
Speeds in gears	1st - 50mph
	2nd - 74mph
	3rd - 99mph
Standing quarter	14.64 secs/91.18mph
Fuel consumption	48mpg

a road-going XR750, it owed far more to the Sportster. XR heads were used on bigger iron barrels and a modified Sportster crankcase. The result was electrifying performance in a relatively light and nimble package. According to the figures, the XR could reach 60mph from a standstill in less than five seconds and do the quarter mile in 12.88 seconds. To keep things in perspective, it still only had 70bhp, and was no match for the Japanese hypersports bikes. But it was good for image.

*   *   *

On average, Harley-Davidson had made a major change to its big V-twin about once every decade. The first one took care of the 1910s, the IOE 74, the '20s. The 1930s and '40s were shared by the side-valve VL and Knucklehead. The Panhead was a long runner, from late 1940s to mid-'60s. By 1984, its successor,

parts were omitted to produce an entry-level bike for just under $4,000. It was a direct response to the familiar complaint that

Harleys were getting too expensive. The XR1000 on the other hand, was Harley's new performance flagship. Ostensibly

TOP LEFT
Modern Harley riders spend a lot of money on their bikes but still prefer tents to hotels

BOTTOM LEFT
For many customizers, this is the ultimate. A bike by Arlen Ness

TOP RIGHT
FXS Lowrider was a factory custom but for some it's just the start. Dave Kitchener's 1982 Shovelhead, with paint by Baz

BOTTOM RIGHT
Pink and chrome actually go together quite well, though for this bike's owner the shiny bits serve merely to back up the paintwork

the Shovelhead, was old and tired, having been in production for nearly 20 years. So when the Evolution appeared, it was not a moment too soon. There have been suggestions that the Evo was a purely post-AMF engine, but the first prototypes were actually running in 1978. One heartening move was that the

1983 FLHTC

SPECIFICATION

Engine	Air-cooled, 45-degree V-twin, OHV
Cylinder heads	Aluminium alloy
Cylinder barrels	Aluminium alloy
Bore x stroke	88.8 x 108mm
Capacity	1340cc
Compression rate	8.5:1
Power	71.5bhp @ 5,000rpm
Torque	82 ½lb ft @ 3,600rpm
Carburettor	Keihin 38mm
Lubrication	Dry sump
Ignition	Electronic, breakerless, with two-stage advance
Drive	Primary - Duplex chain Final - enclosed chain in oil bath
Clutch	Dry, multiplate
Gearbox	Five-speed constant mesh
Gear ratios	1st - 10.45:1
	2nd - 7.13:1
	3rd - 5.17:1
	4th - 3.98:1
	5th - 3.22:1
Suspension	Front - Telescopic forks, 4.6in travel Rear - Swinging arm, 3.6in travel
Brakes	Front - Twin discs, 11 ½in dia Rear - Disc, 12in dia
Tyres	Front - MT90-16 Rear - MT90-16
Weight	762lb
Wheelbase	63in
Seat height	30 ½in
Fuel capacity	5 gallons
Oil capacity	4 quarts

Performance:
(FLHTC tested by *Cycle World* Nov 1983)

Top speed	96mph
Speeds in gears (calculated at 5,500rpm)	1st - 38mph
	2nd - 56mph
	3rd - 78mph
	4th - 101mph
Standing quarter	14.90 secs/86.62mph
Fuel consumption	47mpg

1986 XLH 1100 Sportster

SPECIFICATION

Engine	Air-cooled, 45-degree V-twin, OHV
Cylinder heads	Aluminium alloy
Cylinder barrels	Aluminium alloy
Bore x stroke	85.1 x 96.8mm
Capacity	1101cc
Compression ratio	9:1
Power	62bhp @ 6,000rpm
Torque	64lb ft @ 4,000rpm
Carburettor	Keihin 34mm
Lubrication	Dry sump
Ignition	Electronic, breakerless
Drive	Primary - Triplex chain
	Final - Chain
Clutch	Wet, multiplate
Gearbox	Four-speed constant mesh
Gear ratios	1st - 10.00:1
	2nd - 7.29:1
	3rd - 5.49:1
	4th - 3.98:1
Suspension.	Front - Telescopic forks, 7.6in travel
	Rear - Swinging arm, 3.0in travel
Brakes	Front - Disc, 11.2in dia
	Rear - Disc, 11.2in dia
Tyres	Front - MJ90-19
	Rear - MT90-16
Weight.	490lb
Wheelbase	59in
Seat height	30in
Fuel capacity	1.8 gallons
Oil capacity	3 quarts

Performance:
(XLH 1100 tested by *Cycle World* Dec 1985)

Top speed.	104mph
Speeds in gears (calculated at 6,100rpm)	1st - 46mph
	2nd - 62mph
	3rd - 83mph
Standing quarter	13.56 secs/97.50mph
Fuel consumption	55mpg

project apparently began after a close examination of warranty claims.

But as its name implied, the Evolution twin (also known as the V-2 or Blockhead) was just that - no radical changes. The valves were still pushrod operated, and there were still just two of them per cylinder with just one carburettor to supply the whole engine. The bottom end was hardly changed and even the bore/stroke dimensions were the same. But having said that, nearly everything from the base gasket upwards was new. There were alloy barrels with cast iron liners and alloy heads with much narrower valve angles and less convoluted ports. Everything was held together by four long through-bolts rather than separate bolts for the heads and barrels. A new lightweight valve train allowed a safe 6,400rpm and the Evo's side squish combustion chambers allowed a higher (8.5:1) compression ratio without pinking. Improved oil drain from the heads reduced oil consumption, and the flat-top Mahle pistons were lighter than before.

In short, the V-2 was more powerful (10%) than the Shovelhead; lighter (by 20lb), more torquey (15%) and less maintenance-intensive. At first, it came only in 80-inch guise, fitted to five of the fourteen 1984 bikes. Perhaps more important was the fact that it had been five

RIGHT
An all-black bike doesn't always stand out among the pinks and metalflakes, but this 1991 FXRS is just as personal a statement as any of the preceding bikes, perhaps more so

OPPOSITE
Well-used Evo, with typical luggage equipment.

years in the making - this time, Harley-Davidson was determined to get it right, and they did. Unlike most other new Harley engines, there were no recalls, no hurried dispatch of modified parts to the dealers; and by and large, there were no disgruntled customers either. The Evo seemed to strike the right balance between modern and traditional technologies. And if some Harley owners considered the latest bikes a little tame, there were always options like the 1984 Softail. Apart from the cunningly-hidden rear dampers, to give an authentic hard tail look, the Softail deliberately stuck to a four-speed gearbox and rigidly-mounted engine, to give that authentic vibration.

The press liked the Evo too. *Cycle World* tested the new FLHTC in November 1983. (To translate, the letters FLHTC stand for FLT Tour Glide with the FLH's fairing and luggage, plus a 'C' to denote the new engine.) It was a second quicker than the Shovelhead over the quarter mile and 'pulls eagerly from idle to the 5,500rpm red line.' It was, they concluded, 'modern yet familiar...proof that the eagle still soars.'

One thing became abundantly clear as the '80s rolled on. Harley-Davidson was beginning to make quite an art of parts bin engineering - producing 'new' bikes from different combinations of existing parts. A fairing here, different style of luggage there, yet another letter on the model designation. But in truth, the entire mid-'80's line-up was based around two engines (Sportster 997cc and Evo 1340), rubber or rigidly mounted, four- or five-speed gearboxes and a plethora of alternative wheels, tanks and seats to tell the bikes apart. Take the FXRDG, which surfaced in 1984. Its only real unique selling

1989 Springer Softail FXSTS

SPECIFICATION

Engine	Air-cooled, 45-degree V-twin, OHV
Cylinder heads	Aluminium alloy
Cylinder barrels	Aluminium alloy
Bore x stroke	88.0 x 108.0mm
Capacity	1340cc
Compression ratio	8.5:1
Power	70bhp @ 5,000rpm
Torque	80lb ft @ 4,000rpm
Carburettor	Keihin CV 38mm
Lubrication	Dry sump
Ignition	Electronic, breakerless
Drive	Primary - Duplex chain
	Final - Toothed belt
Clutch	Wet, multiplate
Gearbox	Five-speed constant mesh
Gear ratios	1st - 10.93:1
	2nd - 7.45:1
	3rd - 5.40:1
	4th - 4.16:1
	5th - 3.37:1
Suspension	Front - Leading link sprung forks, 3.9in travel
	Rear - Twin dampers, 4in travel
Brakes	Front - Disc, 11 1/2in dia
	Rear - Disc, 11 1/2in dia
Tyres	Front - MH90-21
	Rear - MT90-16
Weight	630lb
Wheelbase	65in
Seat height	26 1/2in
Fuel capacity	4.6 gallons
Oil capacity	3 quarts

Performance:
(FXSTS tested by *Cycle World* Feb 1989)

Top speed	116mph
Speeds in gears (calculated at 5,200rpm)	1st - 36mph
	2nd - 53mph
	3rd - 73mph
	4th - 95mph
Standing quarter	14.15 secs/93.75mph
Fuel consumption	48mpg

feature was a solid disc rear wheel and lots of chrome. Otherwise, it was another Evo-engined bike with rubber

mounting and five-speed gearbox in the standard FXR frame. No other motorcycle maker had invested so heavily

ABOVE
Triple piston Billets for this Softail

BELOW
Two Heritage Softails, and two different approaches to customizing

in this building block strategy and none has been so successful. It was not only the Evo, but improved quality and productivity in general that was the secret of Harley-Davidson's 1980s turnaround.

Not that it had all been smooth sailing since the management buyout. In 1983, Harley's share of the U.S. 850cc plus market slumped to only 23.3 per cent, and the company was chronically short of cash. Two years later, its main bankers, Citicorp, pulled out, and Harley-Davidson was only days away from bankruptcy when a new backer was found. But when it did come, the turnaround was rapid - 1988 saw a $27 million profit and

market share of 46.5 per cent. There were two main reasons; going public in 1986 enabled dealers, the public and investors to buy Harley-Davidson shares, which brought a huge influx of much-needed capital. The company was also able to evolve its Productivity Triad (Just-in-time inventory, Employee involvement and Statistical operator control) which increased productivity and reduced waste. Meanwhile, quality improved by leaps and bounds.

There were some genuinely new models too. In 1986, the Evolution Sportster arrived. Although by 1985 all the other bikes had acquired the 1340cc Evo, the Sportster had to

struggle on with the old iron barrel 997. It was hardly surprising that the well-received Evolution should down-size to suit the baby Harleys; but to 883cc? There was good reason; in fact there were several. The original entry level XLX had crept up in price, and Harley-Davidson needed an excuse to price the bike down to tempt the first-time buyers. Also, with Harley-Davidson virgins in mind, 883cc meant a lower insurance grouping. An 883 Evolution would be just as powerful as a one litre Shovelhead, and finally, '883' hit just the right nostalgic note.

In keeping with the entry-level aspirations, the gearbox was four-speed, the engine rigid and the drive by chain, not belt. The reward was a $3,995 price tag, $700 less then the old XLX. Judging by the

number of 883s seen at a recent HOG rally near London, the bike has certainly succeeded in bringing new people into the Harley fold. It was not particularly fast, and the average FLH Shovelhead man would dismiss it as a 'Jap Harley', but many of those first-time buyers later traded in their 883s for something bigger, producing a bigger profit margin.

A few months later, there was an 1100cc version, to round out the Sportster range and complete Harley-Davidson's new engine line-up. Apart from 8.9mm extra across the bores, the XLH 1100 was mechanically identical to the 883. All the usual Evo credentials were there - alloy top end, narrower valve angle and more efficient porting. Also like the 883, the engine was not rubber mounted, and *Cycle World* pronounced it a bit

smoother than the old engine at either side of the rev range, but

just as bad in the middle. Still, the whole point of the 1100 was performance - it kept at least some of the 'Sport' in Sportster. Of course, it was leagues behind Japanese bikes with the same pretensions, but that did not seem to matter any more.

Within a couple of years the XLH 1100 had grown into a 1200 - the 74 was back again! A bigger carburettor helped to bring 12 per cent more power and 10 per cent extra torque, but it was not until 1991 that the 883 and 1200 Sportsters acquired the five-speed gearboxes and belt drives to make them thoroughly modern Harleys.

There was, of course, a powerful nostalgia which helped maintain the Sportster's, and indeed all the Harleys', popularity. The success of the first 1984 Softail (it was Harley-Davidson's best-selling bike that year) had not gone unnoticed. Why not take this to its logical conclusion and deliberately design bikes with a distinct feeling of times past? Harleys have always had a classic, timeless look about them, but this could be further enhanced by borrowing specific styling features from long-dead models.

So the first Softail was followed in 1986 by the Heritage Softail. The post-war Hydra-Glides were their inspiration, with their rigid rear ends and big fat forks. On the Heritage, the 'rigid' tail harboured two gas dampers lying horizontally under the gearbox, while the authentic fork shrouds covered a couple of Japanese Showa units. A wide-valanced front mudguard plus suitable paint job completed the look. The Heritage was another success, proving that there are always people willing to pay extra for the right look, even if it is not quite authentic.

But the ultimate nostalgia-

TOP LEFT
There are Aero spun aluminium wheels at both ends, with four-pot Billet calipers. Those rear shocks are by Fournales and the swinging arm is a Ness Twin Rail

LEFT
This 1340 has been enlarged to 1490, backed up by an S & S crank, con-rods and pistons. The carburettor is S & S too, and the camshaft a Crane 286.

BOTTOM LEFT
Owned by Nick Holmes, built by Dean Battistini, with paint by Terry and Tricksey, there is a beautiful simplicity about this FX

TOP RIGHT
Evo-mounted officer pauses for lunch at Daytona

BOTTOM RIGHT
As with all good custom jobs, it's the details that impress, such as the way the mini speedo and tacho are mounted unobtusively below the bars

Harley was yet to come. The Springer Softail appeared in 1988, near-identical to other Softies apart from the return of the Harley-Davidson leading link sprung fork. It really was very similar to the original which had not graced a factory bike for nearly 40 years. Harley-Davidson claimed that the new version had been subjected to extensive computer-assisted design.

We also know that, as the '80s gave way to the '90s, Harleys had become hip. Across the Western world, RUBs flocked to buy V-twin style statements and even today, the bubble shows no sign of bursting.

Perhaps more important than any of these factors is that the company has learnt to listen. It has recognized that while buyers want *the look*, they want reliable electrics as well. Hence came the Fat Boy in 1990, a smoother, sleeker FXR, the latest stylized Harley and the Dyna Glide the following year with new frame, new two-point rubber mounting system and repositioned dampers. When all the talk of legends is set aside, Harley-Davidson is surviving by giving its customers exactly what they want, just as the four original founders did in 1903.

*   *   *

Unfortunately, it still had less than four inches of travel, and part of the package was a very skinny front tyre which was not really up to the job of keeping a 630lb motorbike stable on wet roads. Not many were sold outside the United States, but inside it attracted quite a following and became a permanent part of the range.

We come to 1990, and Harley-Davidson is prospering. There is a 21 model range; production is up to the 50,000 plus of AMF days, but this time there are customers for every single bike. In fact, demand now exceeded supply, and there had to be a strict quota system. The United Kingdom, for example, was allowed about 1,900 Harleys in 1990, yet there were around 20 unofficial dealers, plus numerous individuals, importing bikes to eager customers.

Why this great success? We know that Harleys were now modern where it mattered - clean, reliable and oiltight - that their nostalgia quotient had been fully exploited by a factory that knew exactly what it was about.

Dave Barr has no legs below the knee. He lost them while serving with the South African Army in Angola. But this has not stopped him from riding his 1972 Super Glide around the world. No major back-up, no sponsorship; just himself, artificial legs and the bike. After a long military career, which included service in the U.S. Marines and other forces, Dave returned home to California to

TOP LEFT
Mike Harding's '92 Heritage Softail,
owned from new

CENTRE LEFT
This really is an Evo engine, but the
owner had Panhead rocker covers fitted
to try to individualize it

BOTTOM LEFT
Ingenious paint job by John Spurgeon.
The four cylinders, two each side, show
Knucklehead, Panhead, Shovelhead
and Evo - a lovely idea!

RIGHT
Less elaborate customizing on Dave
Barr's Super Glide, but then it has
racked up over 150,000 miles

BOTTOM RIGHT
The state of the art 1993 Electra Glide
in Mandarine

recuperate. He also needed to overhaul his Harley, which had lain unused for seven years. A couple of minor changes were necessary to make it compatible with his new legs, and in 1983 Dave took the bike back to Africa.

The idea of biking round the world grew gradually - Dave had been inspired by the example of Douglas Bader, the World War II Spitfire pilot who lost both his legs in a flying accident. He was determined to raise awareness to the plight of the disabled - to show what they were capable of doing - and riding his Harley round the world seemed a good way to demonstrate this. He had owned the Super Glide from new and had already covered over 150,000 miles on it. When I met him in London in the summer of 1993, he had added another 70,000 on his global trip. The battered red Shovelhead had obviously seen a lot of life.

His journey began in Johannesburg on 12 September 1990, the bike laden down with spare parts, tools and an extra 24 litres of fuel. Dave's own lugguge was modest by comparison - a little gas cooker, bowl and spoon; not much in the way of food or creature comforts. Crossing Africa was tough. Bad roads and deep sands caused many falls, but floods were to be an even bigger problem. There was often no way of knowing how deep the water was, or how many potholes lay hidden. He was almost drowned once when the bike keeled over and landed on top of him. He was just about able to keep his mouth above water level and hold on until a couple of villagers came along to lift the Harley off. Dave told me, 'I was having to start the Harley by shorting it across the starter terminals with a screwdriver by this time, but mud or no, it would just fire up every time.'

Not that the bike was an absolute paragon of reliability. There were the inevitable punctures, leaking valves, snapped primary belts. The Glide had been converted to belt drive, which Dave considered essential: 'If I hadn't had a belt drive I wouldn't have made it past Zaire.' Four primary chaincases had been smashed in those 70,000 miles. In fact, mechanical problems figured highly - the engine had to be rebuilt at least three times, countless parts had broken and had had to be rewelded in village workshops, army depots, wherever help could

be found. But it kept going and Dave never really doubted that his bike would see him through.

After his African crossing, Dave began to explore Europe, then worked for a time, in order to raise money, at Tiger Cycles in London. He also began to give talks to disabled groups - in particular at the Cheshire Homes, a charity for disabled servicemen. This was to be a recurring theme throughout the trip and he was to address veterans of the Afghan war in Russia as well as disabled civilians in China. Dave Barr has probably spoken to more disabled people than anyone else. Exploration of Europe, Scandinavia and the Arctic

Circle followed, with the benefit of some much appreciated help from local bike clubs.

The next lap entailed shipping the bike across to the United States. Far from being an easy part of the trip, Alaska had to be tackled, and the Harley seems to have had its share of electrical problems. Then all the way back to California and his mother's home in Bodfish. You get a glimpse of the man's great humanity when it was time to leave again: 'It is always great to arrive home, but when it is time to say goodbye and leave behind the ones you love it is a bitter experience indeed...I was on the road again and no matter how painful a parting is, with the

wind in my face, the open highway ahead and the machine pounding away underneath me, my spirits lift as I begin another great adventure.'

Down through Mexico and into South America, Dave was to encounter problems with bad drivers. Attempting to overtake a bus uphill, with a truck bearing down in the opposite direction, the Harley decided to lose power: 'I looked down to see that the rear spark plug wire had come off, so in desperation I grabbed the wire and plug and became a human conductor. As the machine picked up power again, so did I. My eyes must have lit up as I passed the truck - I was truly the electric man!'

Despite such adventures, he made it to Tierra del Fuego, at the very southernmost tip of the Americas, after an interlude with the Brazilian police who generously donated a new set of crankcases. Rebuilt, the bike was shipped to Hong Kong. Then it was up through China, across the Gobi Desert, across Mongolia, Siberia to Moscow, and finally back to Europe, England and Tiger Cycles once again.

The pictures of Dave's bike were taken just as he was about to crate it up for shipment to Australia, the final leg. Before he left he made it quite clear that the journey was not intended as a celebration of motorcycling in general or even as homage to Harley-Davidson in particular, but as an attempt to gain recognition for the needs of disabled people all over the world and as an embodiment of his own personal philosophy; 'Health is a privilege, not a right.'

ABOVE
One man, lots of luggage. A '72 Super Glide and 70,000 miles into a round the world trip

Acknowledgements

No book is ever completed without the help and advice of a great many people. So thanks to all the Harley riders who allowed us to photograph their bikes - Richard Beckett, Nick Holmes, Mike Harding, Mike Wilks, Smokey, Barry Rhodes, Mick Wright, Bernie Stafford, Brian Barrett, Pennie Lennon, Simon Day, John Low, Kenny Acton, Ken Goldsbury, Albert Remme, Derek Frapple, Keith Fulbrook and everyone else. Thanks also to Regency House Publishing for taking on the project.

Should you require more in-depth coverage, can recommend *Harry Sucher's Harley-Davidson: The Milwaukee Marvel,* which gives good coverage of company politics and competition history. *Inside Harley-Davidson* by Jerry Hatfield is a year by year technical history (up to 1945) and Allan Girdler's *Harley-Davidson: The American Motorcycle* provides some useful insights. Finally, Peter Reid's *Well Made in America* tells how the buy-back team turned Harley-Davidson round in the 1980s.

Peter Henshaw
October 1994